THE ERWIN NINE

Hilda Britt Padgett

Cover Design by David Dixon

The Overmountain Press
JOHNSON CITY, TENNESSEE

Cover art for **The Erwin Nine** includes a print titled "Black Thursday" by Art Shultz. It is reproduced with permission of The Boeing Company.

This book is dedicated to all the Unicoi Countians who served during World War II, and especially to my husband, Sterling Padgett, who volunteered and spent twenty years in the United States Navy.

Acknowledgment

I want to thank my cousin, Mary Gail Stallard, who helped me with the organizing and editing of the material for this book.

Preface

On Saturday afternoon, August 17, 1991, I received a call from my son, Charles (Chuck) Padgett from Huntsville, Alabama. He had just received his latest *Erwin Record* which carried a story by Carole Crawford about nine Erwin, Tennessee, men who had been in Stalag Luft IV during World War II. Chuck was amazed and said that he had never heard the story before. He said it was a "Believe It or Not" sort of thing. He was so excited! He wanted me to write a book about it. I jokingly said, "Yeah, sure, I can write a book." He asked if I knew any of the men. I told him that two lived within two blocks of us, and he already knew George Hatcher, who used to be our neighbor.

At that time five of the men lived in Erwin, one in Johnson City, Tennessee, and one in Columbia, Tennessee. Two were deceased. Chuck was so convincing, and he mentioned to me my strong interest in local history. This story is certainly local history. The fact that he had never heard of "The Erwin Nine" made me realize that many have not heard of this unusual happening.

I feel it would be good to have all nine stories in one book, all the memories and mementos put together, and to have the book placed in our local and area libraries.

Introduction

Located in the beautiful mountains of Upper East Tennessee, the town of Erwin and Unicoi County have many things of which to be proud. One of the most unusual stories to come from this small town of 3,350 people occurred during World War II. Nine Army Air Corps servicemen from Erwin were, within a seven-month period, captured by the Germans and placed in the same concentration camp, Stalag Luft IV, located near Grosstychow, Poland.

What kind of town produced these Tennessee Volunteers? Was there any special reason for having so many men and boys enlist? Was it that old independent mountaineer spirit that said we would not stand for other countries to attack our United States? Whatever the reason, we can be proud of all the men and women who served.

This book is about "The Erwin Nine" who were in Stalag Luft IV. We want people to remember how it was when these boys were making bombing runs over Nazi Germany. And remember, at that time some were just boys. They all enlisted—none were drafted.

Unicoi Countians have always answered the call to serve their country. Ten died for it in World War I. During World War II, approximately 2,400 men and women from Unicoi County served. At that time, the population of the county was only 14,428. Eighty-three of these men died while in service. Four men were lost during the Korean Conflict, and thirteen men gave their lives in Vietnam. Fortunately, there were no casualties during Operation Desert Storm, although approximately 120 Unicoi County men and women served in the Gulf War.

On Memorial Day, our local Boy Scout troops put American flags on the graves of servicemen and women. We see many flags flying at that time.

Erwin was just a small mountain village at the turn of the century.

The town began to grow about that time because a railroad was being built through the county. When the Carolina, Clinchfield & Ohio railroad began operating in 1908, many families moved to Erwin from Southwest Virginia and Western North Carolina. Most of these people were fourth and fifth generation Americans whose ancestors were early settlers of Appalachia.

To show how intertwined the people of our town are, I must tell this. Although I am not "blood kin" to any of The Erwin Nine, I am connected to four of them. Richard Edwards's sister is married to my husband's brother. Dick Franklin's aunt was married to my uncle. Stan Norris's uncle was married to my aunt. And Clyde Tinker's wife is a sister to my aunt.

By 1940, the General Offices and all the repair shops of the Clinchfield Railroad were located in Erwin, making the railroad the largest employer in the county. Southern Potteries, which specialized in hand-painted dinnerware, employed about 1,000 people. About half of that number were women who did the delicate hand painting.

Unicoi County had one high school and twenty grade schools. The grade schools were grades one through eight. Two were located in Erwin, and eighteen smaller rural schools were spread throughout the county.

Growing up in Erwin in the late '30s and early '40s was great. It was a time of easy living, but there was always something to do. One of the favorite spots for the young people was Willow Park Swimming Pool. Larger than olympic size, the pool was located in the Canah Chapel area, alongside Indian Creek. The pool was fed with water from Indian Creek, with an inlet and an outlet, so the water constantly flowed and was purified.

Another swimming place was in Rock Creek Park. A large pool had been dug out and was constantly fed by mountain springs. The water was icy. Rock Creek Park is about three miles from Erwin, and most of that uphill. We usually pushed our bicycles to the park, but it was great coming home, coasting all the way to town. There were many swimming holes along Indian Creek—the Blue Hole, the Dave Erwin Hole, Padgett's Dam, Hatcher's Dam, and Pickering's Dam.

One way the youngsters had of making a few cents to buy candy or go to the "show" was by selling pint liquor bottles to the local bootleggers. You could get two cents for a bottle. A walk up or down the alley often turned up a bottle or two.

We had two theaters, the Lyric and the Capitol, where serials such as *Flash Gordon, The Lone Ranger, The Green Hornet*, and *Buck Rogers* really brought the young people into town on Saturdays. In talking with Fred Miller, we both remembered that once while promoting a gangster film, the Lyric Theater had a big car displayed out front. It was supposed to have belonged to Al Capone or some other gangster. Friday night at the Capitol Theater was "Bank Night." Joe Eutsler got a child to draw a ticket from a drum containing names of people who had previously registered. If that person had purchased a theater ticket for that day, he or she won. If there was no winner, the jackpot increased for the following week.

Another time, there was a large preserved whale that was brought into town on a railroad car. For a fee, you could view the whale through a glass partition. Mostly what is remembered about that exhibition is the odor. Such were the thrills of growing up in a small town.

There were numerous baseball and softball teams. Everyone had a chance to play.

Another "activity" that some local boys took part in occurred along the Jackson Love Highway. Before the new highway was built in the '50s, the old, two-lane highway crossed Chestoa Bridge, then there was a steep grade to climb as it came on toward Erwin. During the summer, when watermelon trucks were coming through, the daring young men would wait for a truck, and then one or two would climb aboard as it slowed for the grade. Then they tossed melons to waiting companions, hopped off the truck, and had a feast. I wonder if some of those same boys who tossed melons from a truck ended up dropping bombs from a plane.

Those were the days when adults had time to spend with children. The Catawba Street area youngsters had a friend in O. L. Harvey, better known as "Granddaddy" Harvey to all the neighborhood children. He was a locomotive engineer on the railroad, and everyone around knew when his train was coming in by the distinctive "whippoorwill" whistle he had perfected.

"Granddaddy" Harvey would get a gang of neighborhood children together to go on hikes. We went to the head of Martins Creek, near the top of the mountain where the creek made a falls about ten or fifteen feet high. The water was so pure that you could drink it, and it was always icy cold, even on the hottest day. We hiked to the swimming holes and to the Pinnacle, a Forest Ranger fire tower near the town of Unicoi. Other times he took kids to The Beauty Spot for all night camping.

The Nolichucky River was always good for fishing, either by sitting on the bank with a long cane pole or putting out a trotline across the river to be checked the next day.

The most daring young men weren't on the flying trapeze—they were the ones who attempted to climb The Devil's Looking Glass, a large, sheer rock formation overlooking the Nolichucky River west of Erwin.

Outside activities weren't the only things the young people did. We listened to the radio. There were many good programs. The housewives listened to soap operas during the day, and in the evening, there was *Amos and Andy, Lum and Abner, Fibber McGee and Molly, Jack Benny,* and many more comedy shows. Also, there were many good mystery programs such as *The Shadow* and *Inner Sanctum* with its opening music and introduction with the sound of the squeaking door. Then there was always Saturday night's *Your Lucky Strike Hit Parade* with the latest songs like "Elmer's Tune," "Row, Row, Row," "Tangerine," "Three Little Fishes," "Mairzy Doats," "Sleepy Lagoon," "Tuxedo Junction," "Deep Purple," and of course all the old Glenn Miller favorites such as "Sunrise Serenade," "Moonlight Serenade," and "Perfidia." Then there was *Kay Kyser's Kollege of Musical Knowledge* weekly radio program and *The Lone Ranger, Sgt. Preston of the Yukon, Sky King,* and *Jack Armstrong, All American Boy.*

There were comic books. Today, we wish we had some of those oldies that are now collector's items. And then there were the "Big Little Books." They were about four inches square and two inches thick.

The war clouds gathering in Europe and the Far East soon put an end to these hazy, lazy days of childhood for those of my generation.

The people of Erwin went all out for the war effort. The families of the servicemen especially remember Mrs. Mamie Cook and Mr. Rube Elliott.

Mrs. Cook was the Red Cross director during the war years. Rather than telephoning, Mrs. Cook made personal visits to the homes to tell the families when she received news of the service personnel. Mr. Elliott was the postmaster; he had three sons in the service. He made a special trip to the post office on Sunday afternoons, and if there was mail from overseas, he delivered it personally.

During the war years, service flags were displayed in the windows of homes that had family members in the service. A blue star was shown on the flag for each serviceman or woman. It wasn't unusual to see a three-star flag displayed, as in the case of Fred Miller's family. Those families who lost a loved one had a gold star displayed on the flag.

This was the type of place in which our boys grew up. This was the home of Clyde Tinker, Jim Hensley, Allen Alford, George Swingle, George Hatcher, Fred Miller, Dick Franklin, Stan Norris, and Richard Edwards—*The Erwin Nine.*

The Erwin Nine—L-R: Allen Alford, James Hensley, Stan Norris, Fred Miller, Richard Edwards, Clyde Tinker, George Swingle, George Hatcher, and Dick Franklin.

We are fortunate to have this picture of The Erwin Nine that was taken in July 1945 when all the men were home on leave. Before going to Miami Beach, they were able to get together for the picture.

That incident came about from a conversation between Clyde Tinker and Charles Pugh, another returned Erwin veteran, who was working as a photographer for the *Johnson City Press-Chronicle* and the *Erwin Record*.

Charles and Clyde decided that a story and picture of the returned POWs would make a good article for the Erwin paper. Clyde made the arrangements and got all the men together at the YMCA building on Main Street. Charles took the picture. It appeared in the *Erwin Record* on July 26, 1945.

Six of The Erwin Nine—L-R: Allen Alford, James Hensley, Richard Edwards, Fred Miller, Dick Franklin, and George Hatcher.

In the summer of 1991, the local papers advertised that a B-17G bomber would be on display at Tri-Cities Airport in July. The plane, owned by the Confederate Air Force Arizona Wing of Mesa, Arizona, was the best restored of the eight B-17s still flying in the United States. The bomber was on a fund-raising mission to keep the plane and Confederate Air Force in operation.

Dick Franklin read about the coming event and mentioned it to his next-door neighbor, Carole Crawford, who had previously written articles for the *Erwin Record* about The Erwin Nine. They talked about doing another article entitled "46 Years Later," because it was in July 1945 that all nine POWs had been photographed together after being liberated.

Though two of the men were deceased, six lived in the area. Dick got in touch with the local men and organized a reunion at the Airport. Crawford was there for the story and Charles Edwards (also employed by the *Erwin Record*) for the pictures.

It was a very hot July day at the airport. The Erwin group told the

"Colonel" of the Confederate Air Force why they were there and said they would like to take pictures inside and outside the plane. The "Colonel" said he was afraid that the paying visitors would complain of having to stand in the heat while waiting to go aboard the plane.

The "Colonel" made an announcement over his bullhorn. Instead of complaining, the waiting people mobbed the Erwin men, anxious to talk to them. One man asked if he could take his grandson's picture with Dick, which he did.

The restored B-17 was named *Sentimental Journey*. The painting on its side was of Betty Grable in one of her famous swimsuit poses.

The "Colonel" was very excited to hear the story of The Erwin Nine. He wished he had known about them earlier, so he could have made arrangements for them to fly with him to Lexington, Kentucky, where the plane would be on display the following day.

Crawford sent copies of the article from the *Erwin Record* to the "Colonel", as he had requested, and a copy is now on display at the Confederate Air Force Museum in Mesa.

An article about the reunion appeared in the national POW magazine, *The Ex-POW Bulletin*, and Dick Franklin heard from a man in Atlanta, Georgia, who had been on the boat with him when he came home in 1945.

Nine young men left their homes in a small town and flew off to parts unknown. They all ended up in the same German concentration camp, but each arrived at different times and under different circumstances. They each have their own stories and accounts of what happened, some of which are difficult for most of us to comprehend.

In places, these stories overlap, and at times these overlappings may be contradictory. History will always have such discrepancies. Each of the nine men viewed events from his own perspective, and brought to that viewing his own bias and background. And then came fifty years before this retelling.

Clyde D. Tinker in 1947

CLYDE D. TINKER
Service #14158142
POW #1300

Clyde D. Tinker was born in Unicoi County on September 22, 1910. His parents were John William and Annie Elizabeth McInturff Tinker. His grandparents were James Samuel and Sarah Katherine Jones McInturff and Robert F. and Vinace Claborne Tinker. He had three brothers, Merle, Cecil, and Earl, and two sisters, Pauline and Maggie.

Clyde never liked to talk about his war experiences, and he didn't save his service records. The information for this book has been gathered from different sources.

Thanks go to Leonard Rose of Indianapolis, Indiana, the National Director of The American Ex-Prisoners of War Association. We corresponded many times. He furnished Clyde's service number and POW number, and also provided the Bomb Squadron and Bomb Group to which Clyde had been assigned. In addition, he supplied information about Don Kirby, who had been mentioned by some of the other Erwin men as being with Clyde during his confinement and as having saved his life.

Kirby was in touch by both phone and letter, and was able to fill in the blanks and provide details. He and Clyde were together during most of their service time.

Fred Stallard, Bert Shelton, Val Shelton, and Clyde Tinker in the 1930s

The Erwin men said that Kirby was a big husky fellow. (He would have to have been in order to do what he did!) They thought he had played college football. It turned out that he had played professional baseball with a farm team of the Cincinnati Reds.

During the 1930s,

— 1 —

Sue Shelton, Clyde Tinker, Opal Stallard, Bert Shelton, and Fred Stallard in the 1930s

Clyde drove a truck for the Orange Crush Bottling Company of Johnson City. He hauled Falls City Beer from Louisville, Kentucky, and Hudepohl Beer from Cincinnati, Ohio. Occasionally he made runs to Terre Haute, Indiana, and St. Louis, Missouri.

Clyde and Sue Shelton were married on June 22, 1940, and lived in Erwin. By 1941, Clyde had acquired several trucks of his own and was making regular runs to St. Louis.

He decided to enlist in the Air Corps rather than wait to be drafted, because he felt that he would have a better chance to get the kind of service he wanted. He sold his trucking business and enlisted in 1942.

He received training in Moses Lake, Washington; Pendleton, Oregon; Pyote, Texas; Kansas; and Mississippi; and he received his wings at Tyndall Field in Panama City, Florida.

Clyde was assigned to a crew at Salt Lake City, Utah, and they went overseas in the latter part of 1943. They went by way of Presque Isle, Maine; Goosebay, Labrador; and Iceland, and were stationed at Deophengreen Field near Norwich, England. Their crew was disorganized, and while waiting for a new crew to be made up, Clyde and Kirby flew several missions as replacements in other groups.

They were then assigned to the 730th Bomb Squadron, 452nd Bomb Group of the 8th Air Corps. Their plane was a B-17 named *The 49er*. Clyde was a staff sergeant and waist gunner. A B-17 crew consisted of four officers—pilot, co-pilot, navigator, and bombardier—and six enlisted men—top turret gunner, ball turret gunner, radio operator/gunner, two waist gunners, and a tail gunner.

THE CREW OF *THE 49ER*:
Pilot - Robert Lorenzi - Spokane, Washington - Wounded
Co-pilot - Robert Costello - California
Navigator - William Packer - Chicago, Illinois
Bombardier - Abraham Rosenthal - Binghampton, N. Y - Killed
Radio Operator/Gunner - Don Kirby - Groveport, Ohio - Wounded
Engineer/Gunner - Ed Sweeney - Connecticut
Waist Gunner - Clyde Tinker - Erwin, Tennessee - Wounded
Ball Turret Gunner - Ray Lentz - Toledo, Ohio - Wounded
Tail Gunner - William Strayhorn - North Carolina - Arm shot off
Waist Gunner - Rene Gillman - Chicago, Illinois

On February 8, 1944, the crew flew a mission to Frankfurt, Germany. They were knocked out of formation by fighter planes and fought a running battle, off and on, for several hours before being shot down approximately sixty miles before reaching the English Channel. This was their first mission.

Clyde was hit and knocked down, but he was wearing his flack suit vest and was not badly hurt. Kirby was also hit, and Clyde was able to help him. Thereafter, they took turns checking on each other throughout their imprisonment.

Clyde was the oldest member of the crew. The other members said that it helped having him around when things got tough. Lorenzi, Costello, Packer, and Sweeney got back to England through the underground in France. When Clyde and Kirby were first captured, they were sent to Stalag Luft III near Sagan, Germany. Apparently the Germans had not gotten their prisoner transfer system organized at this time. They later had it very well perfected. The captured American and British flyers were sent to Stalag Luft prison camps. The other prisoners went to Stalags. Only airmen were in the Stalag Luft camps.

The first Erwin men captured did not go through the perfected system of being interrogated at the Dulag at Wetzlar before being sent on to designated camps. The later captives, Hatcher, Franklin, Norris, Edwards, and Hensley all went through the Dulag at Wetzlar before going to Stalag Luft IV.

Information acquired from the War Department states that the name Dulag is a contraction of "durchgangslager," or entrance camp. Dulag Luft had three sections: a hospital at Hohemark, an interrogation center at Oberursel, and a transit camp at Wetzlar. All were located near Frankfurt.

Dulag Luft continued to be a transit camp until liberation on March 25, 1945. After liberation, Dulag Luft was still used as a transit point. It was used to process the ex-prisoners. Seven hundred and fifty ex-prisoners arrived on March 29, and more arrived daily. They were deloused, bathed, clothed, fed, and given haircuts and medical attention by American and British personnel.

Clyde and Kirby stayed at Stalag Luft III for about three months. It was here that Clyde met up with Allen Alford, another of The Erwin Nine. From Stalag Luft III, the prisoners were sent to Stalag Luft VI in Lithuania. Clyde was in poor physical condition during the whole time of his confinement. While at Stalag Luft VI, he was in the lazaret (camp hospital) for several weeks. A prisoner had to be very ill in order to be put into the hospital.

From Stalag Luft VI, the prisoners were taken by train through Königsberg, East Prussia, to Danzig, where they were put on an old Russian ship. About 3,000 prisoners were crowded into the ship's hold. It was a miserable trip that lasted for two days and nights. This was in July 1944. (Two old Russian ships were used to transport the prisoners: the *Insterburg* and the *Masuren*.)

A captain named Pickard was in charge of the prisoners when they arrived near Stalag Luft IV. His family had been bombed out during the early part of the war, and he was very bitter toward the Americans. He ordered the prisoners to run to the camp. Clyde and Kirby were shackled together and could hardly run, plus Clyde was still in poor condition. The guards and guard dogs ran the prisoners through the streets of the town near the camp. (All the Erwin men reported that there seemed to be a guard dog for about every six German guards.) The people of the town lined the street, and they heckled and spit at the prisoners.

Clyde's backpack strap began to choke him, and he passed out. As Kirby attempted to pick him up, one of the guards kept hitting Kirby on the back. Kirby had to lighten his load in order to lift Clyde, so he pulled his own backpack off his shoulders. When the guard came at him again, Kirby swung the backpack and caught the man, just like a good block in a football game. The guard's gun went up into the air and bounced on the cobblestones. The guard and his dog also went up into the air and bounced on the cobblestones! Kirby threw Clyde over his shoulder and ran to mingle with the other prisoners.

About a half mile from the camp, Kirby and Clyde came across a prisoner lying in the road, surrounded by dogs. Kirby asked Clyde if he could manage by just holding on to him. Clyde said that he could, so Kirby hoisted the other man over his shoulder and supported Clyde and made it to the camp. When they got to the camp, they turned the man over to the other prisoners to care for. Clyde and Kirby got into the thick of the prisoners, and Kirby removed his hat and tried to look different. By now Clyde was standing, so when the guards came through looking everyone over to find the prisoner who had knocked down the guard, they couldn't identify him.

The prisoner who had been lying in the road was Hyman Hatton from Brooklyn, New York. Kirby was awarded the Bronze Star Medal for his rescue of Clyde and Hatton.

When they first got to Stalag Luft IV in July 1944, Clyde's group had to sleep on the ground for about three months. The camp had been opened for American prisoners in May but was not yet completed. After three months, they were moved into Lager D with the English and Polish prisoners.

The prison camp had four lagers—A, B, C, and D. Each lager contained ten barracks, a kitchen, and an assembly room behind the kitchen. There were about 2,000 men in each lager. The barracks had ten rooms with eight double bunks in each room and a washroom in the back that had a stove to heat water and take a bath. Two or three men took care of the washroom.

Clyde and Kirby's group left Stalag Luft IV on February 5, 1945, and started on a march that lasted for eighty-five days and approximately 800 miles. The prisoners were divided into groups to allow the Germans to make provisions for feeding them along the way. Clyde and Kirby were separated on the first day of the march—Kirby had escaped. He was later recaptured, but he and Clyde didn't get together again until after the war. They visited each other several times and remained very close friends.

Kirby was a police officer in Columbus, Ohio, for twenty-six years. He said that he had been in some very sticky situations and would say to himself, "Well, Tink, here we go again." That always made things easier.

While on the march, Clyde was put into a group of sick and weak prisoners. This group started on the march an hour earlier each day and ended an hour later. This allowed them to have rest periods along the way.

Richard Edwards said that at one time on the march, he passed Clyde's group which was resting on the side of the road. Richard remarked that he waved to Clyde and walked on—he couldn't stop.

Richard felt that he would never see Clyde again because he looked so bad.

Clyde made it to Stalag 357 near Fallingbostel, Germany. It was here that he and Jim Hensley got together. Stalag 357 was a large international camp. When the Germans were evacuating the camp as the British were closing in, Clyde and Jim hid in the barracks instead of being marched out with the other prisoners. The account of their time at Stalag 357 and arrival at the air base outside Bremen is recorded in the chapter on Jim Hensley.

Clyde never wanted to talk about his war experiences, but often said that his meeting and talking with General Eisenhower was something he would never forget.

They were at the air base outside Bremen for several days where they were deloused, had showers, shaves, and haircuts, and were issued new uniforms. From Bremen, Clyde was sent to England for several weeks of hospitalization to have his health built up before traveling home.

He was discharged from the Air Corps in May 1945. Shortly after

Tinker's Tavern Softball Team
L-R: back row - Clyde Holsclaw, Charles Harmon, Richard Edwards, unknown, and Bill Whitson; front row - Burley Adkins, Charles Jones (batboy), Don Waldrop, Frank Stultz, Louie Moore, and Clyde Tinker.

returning home, Clyde purchased a tavern from Dewey Banks. Tinker's Tavern was located on Carolina Avenue and became a popular place to congregate, especially for the returning veterans. The tavern sponsored a softball team, and we are fortunate to have a picture of the team showing Clyde and Richard Edwards.

Clyde and Sue lived in an apartment above the tavern until 1958 when they purchased a farm in Washington County near where David Crockett High School was later built. They were living on the farm when Clyde died on January 5, 1966.

Interview with Sue Tinker taped in September 1991
Additional information provided by Jim Hensley, Allen Alford,
Richard Edwards, Leonard Rose, and Don Kirby

JAMES H. HENSLEY, JR.
Service #14158015
POW #2973

James H. Hensley, Jr., would very likely have made the Air Corps his career if he had not been a POW. He really loved those planes. But after 126 days of hiding in Holland and Belgium and 292 days as a POW in Germany, he was ready to come home to stay.

Home, of course, was Erwin, Tennessee, where Jim was born on October 3, 1922. His parents were James H. and Martha Elizabeth Buctner Hensley, who came originally from Yancey County, North Carolina. Jim had one sister, Edna, and four brothers: Fred, Vernon, Lyle, and Frank. They are all now deceased.

Jim attended Elm Street and Love Street Schools and Unicoi County High School. He joined the Air Corps before graduating from high school, but received his diploma through the Air Corps.

When he enlisted, his family lived at 231 Third Street. While in school, Jim had worked at different jobs. He worked as a bus boy for Mrs. Belle Morgan at the Rainbow Tea Room, at Coley's Pharmacy as a soda jerk, and at the YMCA, where most of the boys worked to earn their membership.

Jim's older brother Vernon was in the sign painting business in Elizabethton. From Vernon, Jim learned the business. While in high school, he painted "specials" on store windows in Erwin.

Jim joined the Air Corps on September 26, 1942. He was inducted at Camp Forrest, Tennessee. From there he went to Miami Beach, Florida, for basic training, then to Amarillo, Texas, for aircraft mechanics B-17 school. From Amarillo, he was sent to Long Beach, California, for aircraft mechanics B-17 specialists school. After Long Beach, he went to Wendover Field, Utah, for aerial gunnery school.

Next he went to Pyote, Texas, where he was assigned as flight engineer and picked up a crew. They went through three stages of basic flight training. From Pyote, they were sent to Dyersburg, Tennessee, for another phase of training. However, before the training was completed, Jim and several other members of the crew came down with ptomaine poisoning, and the crew was split up. The only members of that first crew that Jim can remember were George Diekoff, the pilot; the

James H. Hensley, Jr.

radioman, Jenssen; and the navigator or bombardier named Fontaine.

Jim especially remembers a time while training with the first crew. They were having a rough training flight, and Fontaine got sick. He asked Jim to hand him one of the "barf bags" they used when they had to throw up. Jim couldn't find a bag, so he handed Fontaine his own hat—which he used. Fontaine threatened Jim with death.

From Dyersburg, Jim was sent to Jackson, Mississippi, for reassignment. One day while at Jackson, Jim passed an officer and saluted. The officer returned the salute, then called to Jim and asked him what kind of wings he was wearing, explaining he had never seen them before. Jim said that they were Aerial Engineer wings. He and the officer started a conversation, and when Jim told him he was just killing time until being assigned to a crew, the officer asked him if he would like to do some flying. The officer told him to pick up a parachute and meet him later. They flew in an AT-6 training plane and made a day of it with touch landings, take offs, and a few barrel rolls. Jim even had an opportunity to fly the plane. He said that was one of the happiest experiences of his service days.

From Jackson, Mississippi, Jim was sent to Salt Lake City, Utah, and then back to Dyersburg, Tennessee, to pick up a crew.

THE CREW:
Pilot - 1st Lt. Charles D. Crook - St. Petersburg, Florida
Co-pilot - 2nd Lt. E. N. Evans
Navigator - 2nd Lt. Roscoe Davis - Deland, Florida
Bombardier - F. O. Joseph Deluca - New York, New York
Radioman - T/Sgt. R. J. Hannan - San Francisco, California
Ball Turret Gunner - S/Sgt. R. A. Cheek - Lawson, Missouri
Left Waist Gunner - S/Sgt. N. R. Williams - Grantville, Georgia
Right Waist Gunner - Sgt. Salvador Chavez - Oklahoma City, Oklahoma
Tail Gunner - Sgt. J. H. Hensley - Erwin, Tennessee
Flight Engineer - T/Sgt. Lou H. Breitenbach - Cincinnati, Ohio

At Dyersburg, Jim was assigned to be a tail gunner. He wasn't very happy about that because all his training had been for an engineer. He was told that once they got overseas he would likely be assigned as flight engineer. He explained that the biggest drawback to the tail gunner's job was the position they had to stay in for seven or eight hours during a mission. The area in the tail of the plane was so small that the gunner had to

Jim Hensley's crew, L-R: front row - Davis, Evans, Deluca, Crook; back row - Breitenbach, Hannan, Williams, Chavez, Hensley, Cheek.

sit on a padded board platform with his legs tucked underneath, almost like sitting on his knees. He had to remain in this position because there just wasn't room to move around.

The cramped position was helped somewhat by the thickness of the clothing that the men wore. They had heavy wool socks, heavy woolen underwear, a heated suit which could be plugged into the electrical system, then flight coveralls, and a fleece-lined flight suit. That sounds like a lot of clothing, but when flying at 32,000-35,000 feet with temperatures of fifty degrees below zero, no doubt it felt good.

Jim's crew went overseas on November 9, 1943. They went aboard the *Queen Elizabeth*, which had been stripped of her former elegance. The ocean trip took five days. They went first to Glasgow, Scotland, next to Nelson Hall, England, to pick up flight equipment, and finally to an air base near Molesworth, west of Cambridge, England. They were assigned to the 360th Squadron, 303rd Bomber Group of the 8th Air Corps.

Jim was able to make a number of trips to London, because when the weather was bad, they could not fly; therefore, they were able to get passes to leave the base. He remembers that even though London had been bombed repeatedly, everything was orderly. Immediately after the bombings, the Londoners were out cleaning up the rubble and boarding up the windows.

Jim particularly remembers his first trip to London. He was with two or three other men just after payday. They got a cab and told the driver they wanted to see London. The driver said it would be expensive, but the boys said that was okay—they wanted the tour. Jim says it was worth it, because the cab driver took them around and pointed out all the special sights.

Covent Garden was one of the places the American GIs enjoyed. It had a huge dance hall, featuring the big bands. When one band stopped playing, another one started up. It seemed that London didn't sleep. There was always something going on, and the British people were extremely good to the Americans.

Jim's crew didn't have their own plane. The crews were rotated on different planes. They were supposed to fly two missions, then have a day off, but sometimes they flew three missions in a row.

Once when returning from one of the raids to Kiel, they were flying at about 30,000 feet. Jim looked over his left shoulder and saw a sky full of rainbows. He described it as hundreds of rainbows that would just pop up and then disappear. He thinks it was caused by the sun reflecting from the vapors of the planes ahead. None of the mission's other flyers mentioned seeing the rainbows. Jim said it was one of the most awesome sights he has ever seen.

The thirteenth mission was on February 22, 1944. They were flying a brand new plane. (The Co-pilot, 2nd Lt. E. N. Evans, was sick and was replaced by 2nd Lt. William Clark of Brunswick, Georgia.) The target was an aircraft factory at Aschersleben, Germany. On the way back to England, Jim's plane was "Tailend Charlie," that is, the last plane in the formation. Being in that position, it was the first plane to be fired upon when the swarm of Messerschmitts came upon them.

One of the engines was shot out, and the plane flipped over on to its side. When the plane flipped, all the ammunition in the box to Jim's right spilled on to him because the new plane did not have a cover for the ammo box. He tried to get the ammo back into the box while watching a lone Messerschmitt that was following the plane. As the B-17 lost altitude, the pilot got it back onto an even flight and slipped into some cloud cover. The Messerschmitt continued to follow, staying out of range of Jim's gun. The bomber pilot had lowered the landing gear so the enemy plane knew they were going to crash-land.

While they still had enough altitude, two of the crew members bailed out. Williams landed in Germany and broke his leg in the fall. He was captured by the Germans. Cheek landed in Holland and was protected and cared for by the Dutch underground until the end of the war.

After crossing the border into Holland, the pilot announced that they were set for a crash-landing. By this time the Messerschmitt had attacked and shot out another engine.

Jim finally got all the ammo off of himself and was able to climb out of the tail turret and get to the radio room, per instructions in case of crash-landing. Chavez was already there.

The plane landed in a field, on the edge of a frozen pond. The right wing tipped over into the pond, shattering the ice. The plane did not catch fire, but was badly damaged as it slid along the ground. Jim was the first one out. He walked along the wing, then into the water, about knee deep. He lost his flight boots when they became mired in the mud. When he got to the bank of the pond, he waited to see if the other men were getting out. All were okay and coming out of the plane. The Messerschmitt made a pass and strafed the men on the ground. Luckily, none were hit.

There was a road to the right of the pond. A civilian man ran down the road and motioned for the men to get away from the plane. They scattered as fast as they could. The men had been instructed, in case of crash-landing, to separate and head for open country where they might find an isolated house. They were already in open country, so they took off in different directions. Jim and Chavez decided to stay together.

They had landed about four o'clock in the afternoon, and it soon began to get dark. Jim and Chavez headed north. Just before it got completely dark, they ran into Lou Breitenbach in a thicket. Breitenbach had his maps all spread out, trying to figure out which way to go. They discovered that they had landed near the small town of Wij Bij Duurstede, Holland.

Jim and Chavez continued on together, cold and hungry. They finally came upon an isolated farmhouse and knocked. A lady came to the door and could see that they were flyers. She was a bit hesitant, but let them come in. Jim said the first thing he noticed was how WARM it was. There was a little girl in the family. The lady fixed sandwiches and tea or coffee for the men. She could not speak English, but when they started to leave, she made them understand that her husband would soon be home, and they should stay. After some time, the husband came home, riding a bicycle. He could speak some English and told them to stay. He then left, and after awhile Jim and Chavez began to get scared, thinking that they would be turned in. They heard a car come to the house. That really scared them, until a man walked in and said, "Welcome to Holland."

The man who welcomed them took them farther into the country. They were taken to a very nice house that belonged to the mayor of the small nearby village. The mayor had gone underground, and there was a housekeeper there taking care of the property. They stayed there that night, and the next night Breitenbach was brought to the house. Jim and Chavez got a kick out of seeing Breitenbach in civilian clothes which weren't the best. At that time, clothing was hard to come by in those countries. They stayed there for several days, and the people found civilian clothing for Jim and Chavez, also.

From this small village, they were taken by car to Utrecht, about twenty miles south of Amsterdam. At Utrecht, they were photographed and had false papers and ID cards made showing that they were deaf mutes. That way they wouldn't be given away by not speaking the language.

L-R: Breitenbach, Chavez, and Hensley while in Holland, dressed as civilians

While in Utrecht, word came that they would have to be moved in a hurry. They had been given razors, toothbrushes, and personal items. So they grabbed their small possessions and prepared to go. They were told that Chavez could not go with them because he was of Mexican descent. At that time, there were no dark complected people in Holland. Chavez was kept in Utrecht for a while. A family rigged a box under their coal bin where he could hide when they thought the enemy might be around. Chavez was later taken to Roermond where he spent the rest of the war hidden at the Oranje Hotel.

From Utrecht, Jim and Breitenbach went by train to Eindhoven. They were given tickets and instructed to get off the train when their contacts got off. They were then turned over to two other men who took them to the home of Marinus Gerard Van Bruggen at Nicolaas Beetsstraat 41. (Van Bruggen was executed by a firing squad at a German concentration camp in August 1944, after years of resistance and helping Allied flyers.)

From Eindhoven Jim and Breitenbach went by train to Roermond. They had been instructed to get off the train, cross the street, go left, and follow the tracks for about a block until they came to an open courtyard. When they got off the train, Breitenbach told Jim he thought they were being followed. They went into the open courtyard and told their contact that they thought someone was following them. The contact instructed them to go back to the street and keep walking. They walked far out into the country before some of the underground people caught up with them and told them that they had not been followed.

The underground contact then took them to what seemed to be an old factory. They spent the night in the basement where coal was stored. They almost froze. It was so cold that they walked the floor all night long. The next day they were taken to a building where a hiding place with food and blankets was made for them. It was still very cold, but not as bad as the night before. The following day they were taken back into Roermond to the place where they were originally headed. They had only had about four hours of sleep in the previous three or four days and were filthy from hiding in the coal bin.

Jim and Breitenbach were taken to the home of the Teuwen family at Godsweerdersingel 23 and were given a room where they were fed and able to take a hot shower with real soap (which was a luxury) before getting into bed. They slept all night and half the next day. When they woke up, all their clothes were laid out for them. EVERYTHING had been dry cleaned or laundered. They stayed with the Teuwens for about five days and were treated as members of the family. The Teuwens were also keeping two British Mosquito pilots and a Dutch youth who was hiding from the Germans.

The purpose in all this movement was that the Dutch underground was trying to get the flyers back to England. Since the English Channel was so well guarded by the Germans, another often used route was from Holland, through Belgium and France, and into Spain where, if captured, their incarceration would be less severe than in Germany. At this time there had been a holdup on the underground line, and the men could not be moved. They stayed in the area of Roermond, Maasniel, and Asenray while awaiting transport to Belgium.

Jim and Breitenbach later stayed with a family named Jenssen in Roermond. The wife's name was Nell, and they had a little boy named Ramey who was three or four years old. Jim and Breitenbach enjoyed being in a home and playing with a child. They especially appreciated the fact that these people took them in. At that time, food was so scarce that it was a sacrifice for a family to try to feed anyone else. Jim learned later that Jenssen was called "Captain Buck" and was high up in the underground movement.

The Jenssens had a special hiding place in their home. There was a trap door in the upstairs floor that led to a space between downstairs room partitions where the two men could comfortably hide. The space was about the size of a closet. During the time Jim and Breitenbach were at the Jenssen home, they did not have to hide because of a house search, but they did hide many times when the Jenssens entertained Germans. Jenssen kept on friendly terms with the Germans to enable him to keep track of the troop and train movements.

After leaving the Jenssen home, Jim and Breitenbach were taken to Asenray where they were cared for by Father Jaques Gerards, a Catholic priest at St. Joseph's Church. They stayed there for about five weeks, the longest they were in any one place. Father Gerards's housekeeper was named Ellie Vissers, and although she did not speak English, they managed to joke with each other. She couldn't understand why the Americans wanted to bathe so often.

Annie and Toon Suntjens, who were close neighbors, often came over at night and played rummy. They had no children, but did have a beautiful Irish setter that Mrs. Suntjens told everyone her husband thought more of than he did her. She was a kind, friendly lady. Mr. Suntjens liked to hunt, and one time when he was lucky enough to get some quail, he invited Jim and Breitenbach for dinner. It turned out to be a feast; they even had champagne.

The parsonage of St. Joseph's Church where Father Gerards hid Jim and Lou Breitenbach

Jim still had his pocket knife and had a talent for carving. He passed the time by carving airplanes for the local people. He was also able to pass the time by reading. Fortunately, Father Gerards had a large library with a number of books in English.

Father Gerards was a jovial person. He thoroughly enjoyed their rummy games. They realized just how much of a jokester he was when they were told to listen carefully to the organ music during the Easter Sunday service. They attended the church, along with the German soldiers who happened to be in the area. Jim and Breitenbach sat in the balcony. During the service, the organist, Maan van Heldens, played "The Star-Spangled Banner." Although mixed in with another song, it was unmistakably the American national anthem.

All the people in the neighborhood wanted to do something for the Americans. Different families would have them come and share a meal. One time, two elderly ladies prepared a special dinner for them. Jim said one of the dishes was some kind of porridge that tasted like sour milk. They just could not eat it. They were so embarrassed because they felt that the ladies had sacrificed to feed them. They were able to communicate enough to let the ladies know it was just something they weren't used to.

Through Father Gerards, Jim and Breitenbach met Antoon Janssen, the young school teacher at the school in Asenray. They spent many hours talking—Janssen wanted to improve his English. After dark, Janssen took them for long walks in the woods, because they were unable to get out during the day for exercise.

After leaving the priest's house in Asenray, Jim and Breitenbach went

L-R: Antoon Janssen, Ellie Vissers, the Irish Setter, Lou Breitenbach, Jim Hensley, Annie Suntjens, and Toon Suntjens in Holland

to Maastricht where a place had been fixed up for them in an old factory building. There they met Colonel Alford and Lieutenant Floyd Martin, with whom they were scheduled to cross the border into Belgium.

One night while they were there, two daring Dutchmen came in and asked them if they wanted to go out for some beer. By this time the men were so bored they were willing to go anywhere. So all four—Jim, Breitenbach, Colonel Alford, and Lieutenant Martin—went to the beer hall with the Dutchmen. They were all dressed as working-class people, no longer passing as deaf mutes, for now they knew a few words of Dutch. At first they were scared to death, but they ended up enjoying themselves even though there were many German soldiers in the beer hall.

From the old factory building they went to a garage where a produce truck was being fixed up to take them into Belgium. The area of the truck bed directly behind the cab was fitted with a false wall. There was just enough room for four men to fit. The top of the truck bed was removed and the four men got inside, then the top was put back on. They were told not to make any noise—not to sneeze, cough, or even breathe loud.

Jim said that even while being scared to death of what might happen, the colonel was always able to come up with something funny. When they were packed into the secret compartment in the truck, the colonel said, "What a way to end it all. We could be machine-gunned and killed

Du Moulin Fernand stands in front of his truck, which took Jim and Breitenbach across the Holland-Belgium border.

in here and no one would ever find us."

The trip across the border into Liege didn't take very long, but they were stopped and searched three times before they got there. Jim says if the Germans had listened very hard, they could have heard his heart beating.

In Liege they were taken to a shoe factory. This was the last time they saw Colonel Alford and Lieutenant Martin. From there they went to a house in an area that had been bombed. Many of the houses were unoccupied after being damaged. This was in a marshalling area of the railroad yards. Jim and Breitenbach were put up in a house occupied by a woman and her daughter and the daughter's son, who was between eight and ten years old. After being there for several days, the son came in one afternoon, white as a sheet, jabbering in French. When his mother was able to make out what he was saying, she told Jim and Breitenbach they would have to get out in a hurry because German trucks were unloading soldiers at the top of the hill and making a house to house search. She led them to one of the unoccupied houses that was boarded up. They got inside and hid upstairs.

The Germans who were making the house to house search were members of the Youth Group. They found Jim and Breitenbach and some other Americans who were hiding in other houses. The date was June 27, 1944. They were all taken into Liege to a prison. While they were in the boarded up house, Jim and Breitenbach had been able to get rid of their forged papers by stuffing them into a stovepipe.

Jim had an unforgettable introduction to German captivity. The prisoners were taken out into a courtyard, and two German guards motioned for them to move over near a wall. Jim thought they meant to go up some steps at the wall. He started up the steps.

A guard grabbed him, pushed him against the wall, and jammed his machine gun under Jim's chin. His head hit the wall with such force that he was momentarily knocked out. A prisoner standing next to Jim caught him and kept him from hitting the ground. He was groggy for some time. Jim and Breitenbach were put in the same cell at the prison where they stayed for one day and night.

From Liege, they were taken to an air base at St. Trond, between Liege and Brussels. At the first interrogation at the air base, Jim was taken to a room and given papers to fill out. He filled out his name, rank, and serial number. When the guard came back in, he told Jim to finish filling out the papers. Jim said that was all he was required to do. The guard took him to a window and showed him a stone wall, pocked with bullet holes. He was told that if he didn't fill out the papers completely, he would be shot for being a spy. Jim said that he was no spy, that he was a shot down American airman. The guard said he had no proof. Jim had his dog tags, which the guard said could be made by the thousands. Of course, the Germans wanted to get the names and information on members of the Dutch underground.

Jim's interrogation was a long drawn out affair. When asked where he got the civilian clothes, he said he had stolen them from a clothesline. When asked who his commanding officer was, he said he had been shot down on his first mission and hadn't had time to remember the names of anyone. Jim was amazed at how thorough the German intelligence system was. They knew when and where he had crash-landed, because he had left on the plane a pair of field glasses that had his name on them.

After a few days at the air base, the prisoners were loaded onto boxcars to be taken to Frankfurt. They passed through Aachen, Düsseldorf, Cologne, Koblenz, and the Rhine River Valley.

When Jim's crew had been making the bombing raids from England, he would check to see what kind of bombs they were going to drop. He always wanted to drop the blockbusters instead of the fire bombs. But when he got to Frankfurt and saw how much damage the fire bombs had done, he was glad that they had carried fire bombs. The city was burned to the ground.

From Frankfurt, they were taken to the Dulag Luft at Wetzlar. They were at Wetzlar for several days. During this time Jim was interrogated over and over with the same old questions. He said it would wear him out, but after so long a time it became routine and he would reply with the same old answers.

At Wetzlar, they were put into boxcars for five or six days and had a miserable trip through Austria and Poland to Stalag Luft IV. This was about July 10, 1944.

Jim was put into Lager A. The barracks rooms weren't too bad. They had a stove that burned some sort of compressed fuel, in brick form, and a table and several chairs.

The men were each issued a blanket that Jim thinks was made of flax. They were told not to wash the blankets, but Jim says that his was so full of sand fleas that he just had to wash it. It shrank up to be the size of a beach towel.

During the first few months at Stalag Luft IV, the food was bad. In the fall, the Red Cross parcels began to come through, and the food improved considerably. They also began receiving clothing packages from the YMCA.

One day when Jim was coming out of the barracks, another prisoner spoke to him and called him "J. H." He knew it had to be someone from home, because the service people always used last names. It turned out to be Fred Miller. Jim said he did not recognize him because he looked so bad. His face was badly scarred, and he had lost so much weight. Jim said that Fred actually gained weight when he first got to Stalag Luft IV.

A room in Lager A had been set up as a sort of dispensary. A doctor was there, and when the Erwin boys from the other lagers came in for sick call, Jim would try to find a chance to talk with them.

One of the prisoners asked Jim just where Erwin was located in Tennessee. When Jim told him, the man said he had traveled through the area many times, but could not remember Erwin. He figured it must be a pretty big place since so many men from Erwin were in the prison camp. When Jim told him the population was only about 3,000, he couldn't believe it.

More Red Cross and YMCA packages came through between Thanksgiving and Christmas. Until then, Jim hardly had a change of clothes. He got more clothes, including an overcoat and high top shoes, which he desperately needed. Before, he had been wearing shoes that he had received in Holland that were too tight for him.

The men were issued eating utensils that included a knife, fork, and spoon. Jim managed to get his knife filed down so it was sharp enough to whittle. He whittled out a whole chess set. When the barracks buddies were getting out of the service, Jim divided up the chess set. He still has the knight that he made.

Sweaters had been issued to the men, but they needed some sort of headwear because of the cold. Jim was able to manipulate a fork into a crochet needle. He had never crocheted before, but he learned. He unraveled the sweaters and crocheted hats for the men.

Jim's group left Stalag Luft IV on February 6, 1945. They were on the march west for forty-five days before arriving at Stalag 357 at Fallingbostel, Germany. Jim and Breitenbach were separated at this time. Breitenbach went by train from Stalag Luft IV to Stalag Luft I at Barth, Germany.

Stalag 357 was a large international camp. Jim and Clyde Tinker wound up being together when they got there. When the British were getting close, the Germans started to move the prisoners again. Jim and Clyde decided they weren't going. As the German guards came in to evacuate the barracks, Jim and Clyde went through a window to the next building, which had already been searched.

The next night, after the camp had been completely evacuated, Jim and Clyde went up to the gate which was still closed. They had been without food and water for over twenty-four hours. With the British closing in, the guards took them to the hospital compound. There were a few more men who had managed to stay in the camp. The following day they were all moved to barracks across the road.

The camp was located on top of a hill and the prisoners were allowed to go down the hill to a farmhouse to get water. One day when Jim and Clyde went for water, they heard a chicken. Clyde told Jim to keep watch. He went into the barn, killed the chicken, and came out with it under his shirt. When the two got back to the barracks, they used the water bucket to boil the chicken. It seemed like it took forever to get tender. From their view on top of the hill, they had seen American planes completely destroy a train down in the valley. As a precaution, Jim was outside staking down strips of white canvas, making the letters "POW," while Clyde cooked the chicken.

A few days before April 19, 1945, the Germans had all left, and a British half-track arrived at the camp. The British soldiers told the handful of prisoners who were still there not to leave the camp; but they did. The men broke into a German warehouse and found guns and ammunition. There was really nothing to shoot, so they shot the windows out of all the buildings.

Then they went into the small town of Fallingbostel at about the same time the British tanks began to arrive. The British tanks had their guns trained on the men because they had weapons. The men began yelling, "We're Americans," and holding their hands up. The first thing the Americans asked was if the British had any food. Several British tanks had pulled up by this time and started unloading food for the Americans.

Some British officers arrived and told the former prisoners to go back to the camp for safety. On April 19, trucks were brought in and the men were taken to an air base outside Bremen.

Jim's group arrived at the air base and was waiting to be deloused when they noticed much activity. Fighter planes were circling the field. Someone asked what was going on, and they were told that General Eisenhower was arriving at the base to meet with General Montgomery. Jim and Clyde weren't impressed. They had not heard much of General Eisenhower in the fourteen months after being shot down.

The general's plane landed, and Eisenhower deplaned and was greeted with much ado. There were a lot of reporters and newsreel cameramen. After the greeting ceremonies were over, General Eisenhower walked across the tarmac to where Jim and Clyde were waiting with the other ex-POWs. He came right up to Jim and Clyde and started asking them questions. This was one of the first POW groups to come out of Germany, and the general asked a lot of questions as to how the men had been treated, where they had been imprisoned, etc. Among other questions, he asked where the men were from. Eisenhower ended by asking if he could do anything for them. Jim said, "Get me home." The general said, "You're on your way."

They spent a couple of days at the air base near Bremen during which time they were deloused, had showers, shaves, haircuts, and were issued new uniforms. It was during this time that Jim and Clyde were separated.

From Brussels, the men were taken by truck to Camp Lucky Strike, near Le Havre, France. Jim sailed from Le Havre on May 1, 1945. His transportation was an old German transport that had been captured during WWI. The voyage was rough, and Jim swore he would never get on another ship. They arrived in New York on May 14, 1945.

The men were sent to a camp in New Jersey for one day, just long enough to be processed. Then Jim traveled by train to Erwin for a sixty-day leave. One of the first POWs to return to Erwin, he was given a warm welcome and was invited by many of the local civic organizations to attend their dinners. One extra special dinner was prepared by Lois Hale. Miss Hale had been Jim's high school teacher when his grades had been barely passing. She had taken him in hand and helped him to boost his grades. She called him "her" boy. Jim said she fixed an elegant meal for his homecoming.

After the sixty-day leave, Jim was sent to Miami Beach. When he first got there, he was put in the hospital for dental work. After a week or more in the hospital, he was sent to North Miami Beach to a place called "The Towers."

At The Towers, they had all sorts of rehabilitation projects, group therapy, etc. Jim enjoyed the workshops in which he made jewelry boxes and a lamp that he still has. It was at The Towers that he was first introduced to plastics.

Jim had been in touch with Mrs. Mamie Cook, the representative of the Red Cross in Erwin. She was helping him to get his records together so he could be discharged. He was disappointed when he was told that he did not have enough points, calculated by length of time in combat, for discharge. He hoped to be discharged early enough to start to school in September. After requesting a transfer, he was moved to Smyrna Air

Jim talks to General Eisenhower.

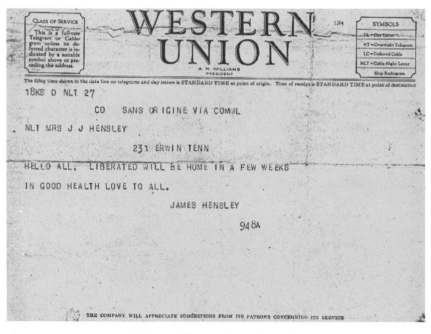

Telegram Jim sent from Brussels

Base near Nashville, Tennessee. After reporting to Smyrna, he asked that his records be checked, and it was found that he did in fact have enough points for discharge.

While at Smyrna, Jim ran into George Hatcher, who told him that Lynn Massengill was at the base. Massengill had been Jim's physical education teacher in high school. Jim looked him up, and they talked all night. Not long after this meeting, Jim was saddened to hear of the death of Massengill as the result of an accident.

From Smyrna Air Base, Jim was sent to Ft. Oglethorpe, Georgia, where he was discharged on September 23, 1945. He enrolled at East Tennessee State College (now University) as soon as he got home. He also started working for his brother Vernon, who had a sign painting shop in Elizabethton. After two quarters, he dropped out of college due to POW related health problems. He continued working in the sign business.

One day, Jim went with his brother to pick up some neon tubing at Yates Sign Company in Johnson City. He began to talk with a man who was working on neon signs, and he thought it looked very interesting. He got all the necessary information about neon training and went to New York City in mid-1946 to attend a six-week course at Eganie Glass Technical Institute. When he came back to Johnson City, he served a three-year apprenticeship with Whitlow Sign Company.

During the time Jim was working for the Whitlow Company, he and Faye Polly Phillips were married. The marriage took place on June 27, 1947, and they made their home in Johnson City.

After the three-year apprenticeship, and no expected raise in pay, Jim quit and went to work in Athens, Georgia, where he worked for Athens Sign Company. From Athens, he came back to Tennessee and opened his own business in Greeneville. Most of his work was in Johnson City, so he moved the plant there. He was in the neon business for about thirty years. He "retired" in 1982, but he still works some and helps out with repair jobs.

Jim and Faye love to travel. They have made two trips to Europe, once in 1962, and again in 1986. The couple was able to visit the places Jim had been to in England and Holland. They also were able to contact some of the people, and children of the people, who had befriended him while he was on the run. They figured that the man who had welcomed them to Holland had been the local doctor. In 1944, the doctor had been the only person in the whole area who had a car. Jim and Faye have made two trips to Hawaii and an extended trip to Alaska.

In 1981, Antoon Janssen and his wife visited Jim and Faye in Johnson City for a week. (Janssen was the young school teacher from Asenray, Holland, who had befriended Jim while he was staying with Father Gerards.) They were taken to many sights of interest in the area, and what really impressed them were the mountains. Having come from the flat land in Holland, they were amazed at the scenery and winding roads.

Jim and Faye have two daughters. Polly Ann, born January 9, 1953, lives in Buford, Georgia. Rebecca Dawn, born April 19, 1957, is married

L-R: Antoon Janssen, Amelie Janssen, Anna Mae Breitenbach, Truus Wijers, Lou Breitenbach, Faye Hensley, and Jim Hensley on visit to Holland in May 1986.

Jim and Faye Hensley   **Polly H. Porter**

to Timothy Shepard, and they live in Snellville, Georgia. Rebecca and her husband have three sons and one daughter: Jamison, Benjamin, Jessica, and Paul.

The Shepard family L-R: back row - Tim, Jamison, and Rebecca; front row - Benjamin, Jessica, and Paul.

Jim lacked three days having three years in the service. He summed up his POW experience like this: It was 125 days in Holland and Belgium, and 292 as a POW. That equals 418 days of frustration, fear, cold, and hunger.

Jim had these figures pertaining to the POWs in the European and Mediterranean theaters of war:

Captured and interned	93,941
Died while a POW	1,121
Returned to the U. S. Military Control	92,820
Alive on January 1, 1988	58,800

Interview with James H. Hensley, Jr., taped on September 23, 1992

ALLEN STEPHENS ALFORD
Service #14156672
POW #1800

In 1944 when Allen Alford was a prisoner of war in Stalag Luft IV, he didn't know the story about his grandfather. If he had, he would probably have thought history was repeating itself. Allen's grandfather, also named Allen Stephens Alford, was born in 1848 and died in 1934, and at age fifteen, he was the youngest man to join the Confederate Army from Putnam County, Georgia. Allen's great-grandfather, John Alford, born September 10, 1815, was the oldest. He was forty-nine.

Allen's grandfather was captured on April 5, 1865, and held as a prisoner of war until the close of the war three weeks later. In 1930 Allen Stephens Alford and John R. Taylor had a reunion in Cochran, Georgia. They had served together as couriers in Company B of Colonel John Blount's Battalion and had not seen each other for sixty-five years.

Seventy-nine years after Allen Stephens Alford was captured by Union forces in Georgia, his namesake was captured by the Germans in Slitz, Germany. He ended up as a prisoner of war in Stalag Luft IV along with eight other young men from Erwin.

Allen's father, Paul Coffer Alford, was born in Georgia in 1883. He married Bessie Edwards Moore, and they moved to Erwin, where he worked for the Clinchfield Railroad in the traffic department.

Allen was born in Johnson City, Tennessee, on September 24, 1922. He had four sisters: Mary Elizabeth, Julia Frances, Sarah Louise, and Rebecca Ann. He also had two brothers: Paul Coffer, Jr., and William Jackson.

He grew up in Erwin and attended grade school at Elm Street and then attended Unicoi County High School. After high school, Allen went to work as a clerk in the accounting department at Clinchfield Railroad in July of 1941.

In July of 1942, Allen was looking forward to a week's paid vacation, which was due to each worker after working for a year. Before vacation time, he was called into a supervisor's office and informed that he was not eligible for the paid vacation because he lacked one day of having enough time in. Needless to say, he was very unhappy. After going home and talking with his father, he went back to work the next day and asked

Allen Alford holds a 30 caliber machine gun.

for a leave of absence so he could join the Air Corps.

At this time, he was only nineteen years old, so he wasn't even registered for the draft. He felt he would eventually have to go, so he may as well enlist and get his choice of services. Allen's brother Jack served in the Merchant Marines during the war. Allen enlisted in the Army Air Corps on September 24, 1942, his twentieth birthday.

After enlisting, Allen was sent to Camp Forrest, Tennessee; Ft. Oglethorpe, Georgia; and then to Miami Beach, Florida, for basic training. From Miami Beach, he was sent to Amarillo, Texas, for air mechanics school. From Amarillo, he was sent to Long Beach, California, to the Boeing plant where the B-17s were built. His group stayed at the plant to watch all procedures in building the plane so they would know all the basic mechanics of the aircraft.

Allen, fourth from left in back row, is shown with fellow students at air mechanics school in Amarillo, TX: John Anderson from Brooklyn, NY, Keith Alfred from Nebraska, Arens from Detroit, MI, Antolich from Pennsylvania, Arnot from Virginia, Clarence Bailey from Brooklyn, NY, Atlas from Brooklyn, NY, Adkens from Knoxville, TN, Gentelle from New York, NY, Brown from Georgia, Atwood from Vermont, and Red Allen from Friendship, NY.

From Long Beach, Allen's group went to Salt Lake City, Utah, where they were assigned crews. Allen's crew then went to Pocatello, Idaho, and then to Wendover, Utah, for gunnery school. From Wendover, they went back to Salt Lake City, then to Salinas, Kansas, where they picked up their plane, *Star Baby*. Though trained on B-17s, *Star Baby* was a B-24. They were in Jimmy Stewart's squadron.

Since it was early winter, they had to fly the plane the southern route to England. Allen called the plane and its several hundred feet of hydraulic lines "a plumber's nightmare" because of all the problems they encountered. Because of a faulty fuel tank, a broken hydraulic line, and bad weather, it took them a month to get to England.

They flew by way of Miami Beach, Puerto Rico, and Natal, Brazil. They had to land on small Ascension Island for repairs and refueling. Next, they traveled to Ghana, then to Dakar, Senegal, and on to Marrakech, and Casablanca. After leaving Casablanca, they got as far as the coast of Spain before developing more problems. So it was back to Casablanca, where they practically had to land in the dark.

Blackouts were in force at this time. They raised the field and persuaded them to turn on the runway lights so they could see to land. Only one row of lights was turned on; then they lost contact with the field and didn't know which side of the runway the lights were on. They did make it, but had to go back to Marrakech for parts. From Marrakech, they finally made it to Southampton, England, and from there to Tibbingham, where their field was located.

They were assigned to the 703rd Squadron, 445th Bomb Group of the 8th Air Corps.

THE CREW OF THE *STAR BABY*:
Pilot - Peter T. Abell - California
Co-pilot - Thomas J. Campbell - Pennsylvania (Campbell was killed on the fifth or sixth mission and several others were co-pilots thereafter.)
Navigator - Raymond A. Parker - California
Bombardier - Walter Yerkes
Radioman - Donald E. Watts - Ionia, Iowa
Waist Gunner/Engineer - Allen Alford - Erwin, Tennessee
Waist Gunner - Lonnie Reeves - Georgia
Ball Turret Gunner - Robert W. Merriam - New Jersey
Engineer - Donald F. Caton
Tail Gunner - Ned A. Dougherty - Turtle Creek, Pennsylvania

The first *Star Baby* cracked up in an irrigation ditch when taking off on a mission with a full bomb load. It was so severely damaged that it had to be replaced. *Star Baby II* was shot up so badly during one of the raids that it also had to be replaced. *Star Baby III* was the plane that went on the thirteenth mission on February 24, 1944. The target was an aircraft plant and cadet base at Gotha, Germany, south of Berlin.

The rallying point for all the squadrons to get together for the big raids was over Ipswich, England. They usually flew out over the cliffs of Dover.

When the plane was shot down, the tail gunner, Ned A. Dougherty,

The crew of the *Star Baby*, L-R: front row - Alford, Caton, Watts, Daugherty, and Reeves; back row - Abell, Parker, Crew Chief Raymond L. Dietrech, Yerkes, and Campbell. Merriam is not in the photograph.

was not aboard. He was on leave. Allen does not remember the name of Dougherty's replacement, nor does he remember the co-pilot's name.

The *Star Baby III* was attacked by ME-210s firing 20mm cannon. The plane was hit and caught fire. The fire was so hot that the aluminum was burning like paper. Half of the 703rd Squadron was lost that day.

The men wore parachute harnesses, and each had a chute, about sixteen feet in diameter, that was to be hooked on to the harness in case of emergency. The chute had a white pick-up strap on one end, and on the other side was the rip cord. When Reeves reached for his chute, he grabbed the rip cord, spilling the silk over the plane. He then grabbed Yerkes, who was ready to bail out.

If he had buckled himself to Yerkes's harness or even hooked his open chute on to his harness, he may have made it. He was holding on to Yerkes's chest. When the chute opened, it was such a jolt that Reeves's hold was broken. As he slid downward, he grabbed Yerkes's foot before he lost contact all together. Yerkes's ankle was broken from the jolt.

Allen bailed out head first, counted to ten, then pulled the rip cord. He thinks that he was at about 17,000 feet. After the chute stopped swinging and had settled down, Allen looked at his watch. It was 2:30 p.m.

He had lost his boots when he bailed out. As he was drifting to the ground, the fighter planes came back toward him. He naturally thought he would be strafed. Instead, they flew around him, causing his chute to be billowed all over the sky. Allen has no idea how much difference this made in where he landed, but he feels that it kept him afloat much longer. It took him about thirty minutes to come down.

As he was drifting to earth, about all he could see was forest. His thoughts were that wolves would get him that night, if he didn't get caught in a tree first.

By the time he got closer to the ground, the forest wasn't so dense. It was farm country. While still several thousand feet in the air, he heard the people on the ground shouting and could even see their faces.

He was drifting down to a small, walled town on a hill beside a river. He later learned that the town was named Slitz. (He was never able to find it on a map.) By the time he landed, he was on the other side of the river. The townspeople couldn't see him because of the hill. He landed in a foot of snow.

After getting rid of his parachute, Allen started down the river, thinking he was getting away from a populated area. Instead, as he rounded a bend in the river, he came upon another small village. He started to cross the hill when he encountered the German civilians who were looking for him. They were armed with farm implements: pitchforks, hoes, etc. The leader seemed to be a woman in her 40s.

They surrounded him until a German soldier showed up, pushing a bicycle through the snow. While the civilians guarded Allen, the soldier backtracked Allen's movements and recovered his parachute and items he had left on the river bank. Then they started to the town of Slitz. The German soldier carried Allen's gear until they got to the town, then he made Allen carry it.

Allen didn't see any people outside the houses in the town. He was taken to a small, unheated, cement block jail and was given some potato salad to eat. There was a straw tick mattress to sleep on. He stayed there for almost two days until he was taken by truck to a train station where four German Luftwaffe officers took charge of him. They boarded a train, the five of them in a compartment, and went to Nuremberg to Gestapo Headquarters. He was there for about forty-eight hours.

During the time he was with the German officers and at Gestapo Headquarters, the Germans kept insisting that he was Lieutenant Edmonds. Apparently he resembled the lieutenant they were looking for.

He wasn't mistreated during this time. The Germans finally decided that he was the person named on his dog tag, so he was sent on to Stalag Luft I, located near Barth, Germany. He was there for less than a week, then he was taken to Stalag Luft III for about three months.

At Stalag Luft III, he was put in the same barracks with Clyde Tinker. Clyde, the first Erwin man to be shot down, had been taken prisoner a few weeks before Allen. Allen said that when he first got to the barracks, Clyde said, "Hello, Jack, what are you doing here?" Clyde had mistaken Allen for his brother Jack.

Allen and Clyde were together during the rest of their confinement at Stalag Luft III and at Stalag Luft VI and Stalag Luft IV. They were separated after liberation, and Clyde got home before Allen.

It was at Stalag Luft VI that Allen saw the old World War I German officers who were also prisoners. They had good quarters, servants, and all necessities. Hitler didn't trust them, so they were kept in confinement throughout the war. It was also at Stalag Luft VI that Allen saw the only brick barracks at any prison camp.

From Stalag Luft VI, Allen's group was taken by train through Königsberg, East Prussia, to Danzig, where they were put on an old Russian grain or coal ship. There were 3,000 prisoners crowded into the ship's hold. The trip lasted for two nights. They arrived near the camp in the summer of 1944 and were forced to run most of the way to Stalag Luft IV.

The food in the prison camp was terrible. The men received two slices of bread per day. It was an awful black bread that tasted like sawdust. They received soup that Allen thinks was made from weeds and kohlrabi. Allen said he swore he would never eat another kohlrabi.

The one hot meal per day was brought into the barracks in a large aluminum kettle. It was then doled out to the men. Allen was barracks chief and in charge of the operation. He said the kettle usually contained soup that was mostly water.

One time the kettle actually contained meat. Allen believes that it was the leg bone from a horse, and it did have particles of meat still clinging to it. There was no way to divide the bone, so the men cut cards to see who would win it. Allen won!

He said the gristle on the bone was, at least, filling. He broke the bone into pieces and scraped out the marrow, which he put into a small can. He used the marrow on his bread. After about a week, the marrow turned rancid and had to be thrown out.

Allen had a good Hamilton wrist watch when he enlisted. His father advised him not to take it with him, so he traded his watch for his father's Elgin wrist watch. Mr. Alford wore Allen's Hamilton all the time that he was gone.

Some of the old-time railroaders will think it sounds funny to say that Paul Alford wore a wrist watch, when they know that ALL railroad men carried pocket watches which were meticulously cared for. Allen explained that his father had the wrist watch for the times his pocket watch was in the shop for regular checkups.

Allen said that whenever he was sent to a new camp, all personal items, such as watches, rings, and other jewelry, were taken. After about ten days, the items were returned, and his father's watch would be given back. He also had an Air Corps-issue watch which was taken. The Germans kept all Air Corps watches.

At Stalag Luft IV, Allen was separated from the British prisoners by a fence. Some of the British had been there since Dunkirk. The British received cigarettes in their Red Cross packages and used them for trade, especially for watches. Some of the men had watches up and down both arms. The cigarettes they received were very good—Sweet Corporal or Canadian brands that were packaged in tins.

One day while talking to a British prisoner who had noticed Allen's watch, a bargain was struck. Allen traded his wrist watch for 7,700 cigarettes! He tried to bargain for 10,000 but had to settle for less. He had to have help to move the boxes.

Allen's buddy Don Watts, who had been the radioman of the *Star Baby III*, was with him at Stalag Luft IV. Watts didn't have anything to trade for cigarettes, so he told Allen he would buy half interest in the watch for $25.00 and pay him after they got home.

So Watts got half the cigarettes.

They used the cigarettes just like money. They could buy a pair of socks or some extra food or even "hire" someone to make their bed. About two months after Allen was discharged, Watts sent him $25.00 for his half interest in the watch.

As the war was winding down and the prisoners were moved out of Stalag Luft IV, Allen and George Hatcher were in the first group to be moved. They were taken in boxcars to a camp near Nuremberg. The trip lasted for several days. They were at the camp for about six weeks. From there, the prisoners were marched to Moosburg, a distance of about eighty miles.

When they arrived at Stalag Luft VII A near Moosburg, they were confined in a large area that had been bulldozed about three feet deep and covered with sawdust. The whole area was enclosed with something like a giant sized circus tent.

When the Germans knew that Patton was on his way to Moosburg, they left the camp. The Germans told the Americans that they should stay within the camp area because the German civilians might still be armed. Instead of leaving the area, the German soldiers went outside the camp and hid in the storehouses. The American prisoners stayed within the camp and put guards, or watches, on the towers until the liberating forces arrived.

The camp was located on the east side of the Isar River from Moosburg. When Patton's forces arrived in Moosburg, all the houses were flying white flags from the highest window in the house. All the flags were exactly the same size, same material, and had the same flagpole. Allen thinks the civilians had been issued the flags shortly before the German soldiers pulled out.

After the Germans left the camp, they blew up the bridge over the Isar. On arriving in Moosburg, the Army Corps of Engineers immediately started to construct a pontoon bridge, which was usable in a very short time. The pontoon bridge could carry the large tanks and trucks, but not regular sized cars and trucks because of the width of the wheel bases.

The prisoners were liberated from Stalag Luft VII A by the 14th Armored Division of the 3rd Army. General George S. Patton, Commander of the 3rd Army, was in the lead tank that broke through the fence surrounding the camp. When the American army arrived a few days before VE Day, they were told by the prisoners where the Germans were hiding. The Americans routed the Germans, a number of which were high ranking officers.

The Germans were marched, single file, up the road to be loaded into trucks. As each was marched by, the ex-POWs were asked if the German was good or bad. The ones who were bad were given very rough treatment.

The Russian prisoners, who were the laborers in the camps, never had any association with the Americans, perhaps because of the language barrier or social status.

As the Germans were marched up the road, the Russian ex-prisoners were standing around the trucks. The Russians were poorly clothed. Very few had shoes—their feet were wrapped in rags. The Germans had on the fancy, high-top black boots with a spit polish shine. One of the Russians grabbed a German officer, threw him to the ground, and pulled his boots off. When he tried them on, they were too small, so he grabbed another officer. This started the exchange. By the time the trucks left, all the Germans were barefoot or in stocking feet, and all the Russians were wearing boots. And most were carrying an extra pair.

The American forces set up field kitchens and started preparing food for the ex-prisoners. Allen said that the fresh baked bread tasted like angel food cake.

After being fed, the American ex-prisoners took over the vehicles that the Germans had left on the town side of the river and drove them until the gas was gone. They had attempted to cross the pontoon bridge, but found it impossible with the smaller vehicles. The town side of the bridge was a mass of abandoned vehicles.

One of Allen's friends at Stalag Luft VII A was David Davage from Louisiana. Allen said that Davage looked like a Kentucky Colonel. He was tall, dignified, had a military bearing, and had let his blond beard grow into a neat goatee. All the men called him "Colonel."

When the ex-prisoners were released and celebrating, they went into Moosburg and helped themselves to the wine and cheese stored in the cellars of the houses. After a few days, MPs were posted at the houses to keep the ex-POWs out. Allen, Davage, and several other men were turned away.

All the ex-prisoners were dressed in prison clothing, so they couldn't be identified by rank. As Allen and the men were turned away, Allen said, "Well, Colonel, it doesn't look like we'll get any wine today." At that, the MP came to attention and motioned for Allen and Davage to step aside. They were then directed around the house to the cellar. Allen didn't report how much wine was consumed, but when they were satisfied, they decided to take some cheese back to the men at the camp.

The cheese was an enormous wheel, covered with cloth, so heavy that they could not carry it—so they rolled it back to the camp. By the time they got there, the cheese was well embedded with gravel.

The ex-prisoners went from Moosburg by truck or bus to Camp Lucky Strike, then on to Le Havre. From Le Havre, Allen boarded a merchant ship for the trip home. He came into New York and said the men almost turned the ship over by rushing to one side to see The Statue of Liberty. There was not a dry eye on the ship.

He then went to Camp Kilmer, New Jersey, on June 13, 1945, for a short time. Soon he arrived in Erwin for a sixty-day leave. He stayed in Erwin for one or two days, then went to Detroit to get Doris Jean Beck, his fiancée, who was in nurses' training at Ford Hospital in Detroit.

Allen stayed in Detroit for one day, then he and Doris Jean returned to

Allen Alford and Doris Jean Beck on their wedding day, July 9, 1945

Erwin. They were married on July 9, 1945. After a one-week honeymoon at Lake Junaluska, they returned for about two weeks in Erwin. Allen and Doris Jean then went to Miami for the rest and relaxation leave that the POWs received. Doris Jean stayed there for two weeks. She remembers the long lines of tables loaded with food, and especially that at the ends of the tables were piles of giant sized Hershey bars. Doris Jean says she embarrassed Allen by loading up on Hershey bars! Allen enjoyed all the food, but was still unable to eat much at one time.

While in Miami, all the men were given physicals, and their records were checked to see what medals they were entitled to. They were also able to make claims for anything that they had lost. Allen had lost a valuable camera and was not reimbursed for it, so he put in a claim for the watch that he had traded for the cigarettes. He was paid for the watch.

Allen explained that when a plane was lost, the area in the barracks where the crew was posted was roped off. A special detail came in and gathered the men's belongings, and all personal effects were packaged and sent home to the next of kin. Allen's personal effects never reached Erwin.

From Miami, Allen was sent to Goldsboro, North Carolina, for about three months. While there, he only had to check in every Monday. The rest of the time, he was free to do as he pleased. Allen hitchhiked home about every week.

He was discharged in December after being in the Air Corps for three years and three months. In December, Allen went back to work at the Clinchfield Railroad offices for a week. He had to report back to work in order to ask for another leave so he could go to college. The railroad granted the leave and gave him credit for the time he had been in service.

Allen entered Milligan College in January of 1946. He graduated in 1951 with a degree in Business Administration, and then went back to work for the Clinchfield Railroad as a clerk stenographer in the Johnson City office. He had been there for less than two years when he was transferred to Spartanburg, South Carolina. Later, he was sent to Augusta, Georgia, and then back to Erwin in 1967. He worked at "The Big Office" as traffic manager in charge of sales.

Allen Alford in 1975

The local people always referred to the general offices of the Clinchfield Railroad, located on Nolichucky Avenue, as "The Big Office." In 1979, when the The Seaboard Coast Line Railroad took over the Clinchfield, all of the business offices were slowly phased out. Allen worked at "The Big Office" long after other departments had been transferred. At one time he had the only office on the third floor. Eventually his office was moved to Kingsport, and he commuted each day.

Allen had a heart attack in 1982, and a few months later he officially retired from the railroad.

The Alfords have five children:

1. Allen Stephens Alford, Jr., married Carol Brandenburg, and they have three children.
   Benjamin Stephens - born May 16, 1974
   Erin Debra - born November 25, 1978
   Emily Carol - born March 7, 1981
2. Teresa Diane Alford married Harry Marion Lewis, Jr., and they have two children.
   Leslie Michelle - born May 5, 1971
   Jason Alford - born December 5, 1973
3. Janice Lynn Alford married Darrel Lindsey Hughes, and they have three children.
   Allen Lindsey - born June 16, 1969
   Travis Darrell - born April 1, 1973
   Sarah Elizabeth - born October 5, 1979
4. Donald Edwin Alford married Judith Pamela Ritter, and they have two children.
   Katherine Suzanne - born May 14, 1980
   Elise Leanne - born May 4, 1985
5. Robert Douglas Alford married (1) Annette Foster, and they have one child.
   Holly Gail - born July 3, 1981
   Robert married (2) Kathy Lynn Effler in 1984, and they have two children.
   Adam Robert - born March 18, 1987
   Hannah Elizabeth - born October 23, 1991

The Alfords live in a lovely home on Rock Creek Road. They have built a large two-story barn between their house and the creek with an enormous fireplace, a modern kitchen and bath, and plenty of room for when the family comes to visit. They also have a cook house near the

Oldest grandson off to Gulf War MASH Unit L-R: front row - Jason Lewis (grandson, now in Air Force), Janice Hughes (daughter), Allen Hughes (grandson), Sarah Hughes (granddaughter), Doris Jean Alford, Elizabeth Mathes (friend); back row - Travis Hughes (grandson), Teresa Lewis (daughter), Harry Lewis (son-in-law), Leslie Lewis (granddaughter).

Oldest grandson off to Gulf War MASH Unit L-R: front row - Sarah Hughes, Leslie Lewis, Doris Jean Alford, Teresa Lewis; back row - Travis Hughes, Janice Hughes, Allen Hughes, Allen Alford, Jason Lewis, Harry Lewis.

Alford family reunion in Plant City, Florida, L-R: front row - Katie Alford, Emily Alford, Sarah Hughes, Elise Alford; second row - Allen Alford, Doris Jean Alford, Carol Alford, Teresa Lewis, Erin Alford; back row - Donald Alford, Stephen Alford, Harry Lewis, Janice Hughes, Travis Hughes, Leslie Lewis, Jason Lewis, Judy Alford, Ben Alford, Adam Alford, Kathy Alford, Rob Alford.

Allen and Doris Jean Alford in 1988

barn where large meals can be prepared. When Allen looks over the family gatherings, with the abundant ·food, he no doubt thinks of those months of hunger in the prison camp.

The Alfords also make the barn available for groups from Centenary United Methodist Church. An often heard phrase is, "We're going to Alford's barn for a picnic."

After forty-three years with the railroad, Allen is enjoying his retirement. He likes to sleep a lot, play golf, and work crossword puzzles. Doris Jean says that he was born to retire.

Interview with Allen Stephens Alford taped on February 6, 1992

GEORGE DAVID SWINGLE
Service #14161347
POW #53165

George David Swingle was born November 15, 1922, in Hamlet, North Carolina. He died on May 20, 1973, in Knoxville, Tennessee. He was the son of James Vincent and Ruth Ervin Swingle. He had one sister, Margaret Ann.

Shortly after George's birth, his family moved back to Erwin, Tennessee, where his ancestors had lived for generations. The town of Erwin was named for George's grandfather, D. J. N. Ervin. When Unicoi County was formed in 1875, the small village was known as Vanderbilt. D. J. N. Ervin gave the county fifteen acres of land to be used to build the courthouse and make Vanderbilt the county seat. The Tennessee Legislature of 1879 changed the name from Vanderbilt to Ervin, in honor of David Jasper Newton Ervin. Somehow a mix-up occurred in the spelling, and the name of the town became Erwin. The Swingles had lived in the Unicoi area since the early 1800s. At one time the village of Unicoi was called Swingleville.

George did not like to talk of his war experiences. His story is told through material and information furnished by his sister, Margaret Ann Swingle; his widow, Evelyn Swingle; and the other POWs.

George attended Elm Street School and graduated from Unicoi County High School in 1941. He entered the University of Tennessee in 1941, just before the beginning of World War II.

After a year at the University of Tennessee, he enlisted in the Army Air Corps in November of 1942. He received training at Moses Lake, Washington; Laredo, Texas; Harvard, Nebraska; and Salt Lake City, Utah.

Swingle went overseas, to England, sometime before December 1943. Some of his service records that have been preserved show that he flew twenty-four combat missions between December 1943 and April 1944.

George was assigned to the 700th Bomb Squadron, 447th Bomb Group, of the 8th Air Corps. Some of the records also state that his station was AAF-126.

The plane to which George was assigned was a B-17 which the crew named the *Jolly Rodger*.

George boards the *Jolly Rodger.*

THE CREW OF THE *JOLLY RODGER:*
Pilot - Ashley M. Guynn
Co-pilot - Ralph E. Lindeman
Navigator - Bud Haidler
Bombardier - Reed Hollister
Engineer - Louis Guenther
Waist Gunner - Bernard Weis
Radio Operator - George Swingle
Waist Gunner - Charles A. Mouser
Ball Turret Gunner - Edward Kucinski
Tail Gunner - Ernie Hernandez

Crew of the *Jolly Rodger* on November 4, 1943, L-R: back row - Guynn, Lindeman, Haidler, Hollister; front row - Guenther, Swingle, Weis, Hernandez, and Mouser. Kucinski was not with the crew at that time.

Combat mission number twenty-four occurred on April 27, 1944. The plane was disabled over Belgium, and George bailed out and landed on top of a house. His leg broke when it went through the roof. It is unknown how long it was until he was captured.

George had kept a map of POW camps on which he had circled Dulag Luft, Stalag Luft III, and Res. Lazaret (hospital) at Stalag IX C, near Obermassfeld. From these markings, it is probable that Swingle was hos-

IN ACCEPTING THIS AIRCRAFT, IT IS OUR
SOLEMN INTENTION TO BRING CREDIT TO HER
AND TO OURSELVES, AND TO CARRY OUT OUR
MISSION WITH THE SKILL AND TENACITY, FOR
WHICH WE PRIDE OURSELVES AS MEMBERS OF
THE 447TH. HEAVY BOMB GROUP AND THE
ARMY AIR FORCES.

PILOT _____ CO-PILOT _____
NAVIGATOR _____ BOMBARDIER _____

ENGINEER _____ WAIST GUNNER _____
RADIO OPERATOR _____ WAIST GUNNER _____
BALL TURRET GUNNER _____ TAIL GUNNER _____

Plane and crew autographs

Crew in flying gear

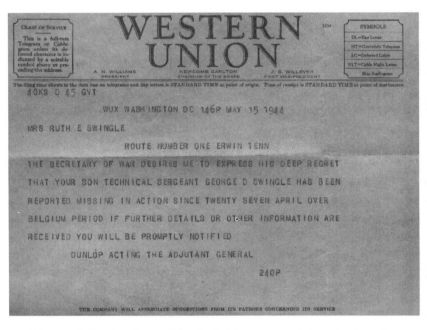

Telegram informing George's family that he was reported missing in action

Telegram informing George's family that he was reported a prisoner

Order blank for tobacco products

pitalized at Stalag IX C. Additional proof that he was there is that one of the papers which has been preserved is an order form for tobacco products to be sent to prisoners. It gives George's address as "Stalag 9-c."

Apparently the German doctors took good care of George while his leg healed. Stan Norris reported that by the time they started on the march, George was walking as well as anyone.

It would seem from the map markings that George went from Stalag IX C to Dulag Luft for interrogation, then to Stalag Luft III before he was sent to Stalag Luft IV. It is known that George was at Stalag Luft IV in late July or early August 1944 when Stan Norris arrived there. They were both in Lager A.

George and Stan became close friends while in the camp. As the war

George's mother, Mrs. Ruth E. Swingle, receives George's Air Medal, with three oak leaf clusters, from Brig. Gen. Ivan L. Farman. Ceremonies were in Asheville, North Carolina, while George was still in prison camp. Other women pictured are, L-R: front - Mrs. Eli Mathis of Johnson City, Mrs. David Purner of Johnson City, and Mrs. Edna B. Swanay of Elizabethton; back - Mrs. Bertha C. Parker of Knoxville, Mrs. Louise E. Lawson of Knoxville, Mrs. Effie M. Allen of Newcomb, Tennessee, Mrs. Pearl B. Ballard of Asheville, North Carolina, Mrs. Martha C. Thompson of Hendersonville, North Carolina, and Mrs. Helen J. Hayes of Beardon, Tennessee.

UNITED STATES
ARMY AIR FORCES

The Air Medal

has been awarded

TECHNICAL SERGEANT GEORGE D. SWINGLE, 14161347

Air Corps, Army of the United States

Citation

For exceptionally meritorious achievement, while participating in more than ten separate bomber combat missions over enemy occupied Continental Europe. The courage, coolness and skill displayed by this Enlisted Man upon these occasions reflect great credit upon himself and the Armed Forces of the United States.

George's Air Medal award

was winding down, Stalag Luft IV was evacuated. The two men were put into the same group for the march that, after many twists and turns, ended up near Lüneburg after their guards had disappeared. There, they met with soldiers of the British Second Army, who directed them to field kitchens where they could be fed. From there, they made their way to Lüneburg. Their adventures from Stalag Luft IV to Camp Lucky Strike are recorded in the chapter on Stan Norris.

It was during the march that George encouraged Stan to attend the University of Tennessee. They agreed to meet and enroll at UT as soon as they got home. The two men were separated from each other at Camp Lucky Strike. Stan made it to Knoxville first. He waited at the Sigma Chi house for George, who arrived about two weeks later.

George graduated from the University of Tennessee in 1948 with a BA degree in geology. He earned his MS degree in geology from UT and then entered the University of Wisconsin to work on his PhD, which he received in 1952.

In 1952 George was employed by the Tennessee Division of Geology as Assistant State Geologist. In the fall of 1953 he resigned that position to join the staff of the Department of Geology at the University of Tennessee. He continued to serve as a consultant to the Tennessee Division of Geology until 1969.

George Swingle

George was extremely active in research and the graduate teaching program at the University of Tennessee. During this time he authored or co-authored forty-nine publications.

George married Evelyn Lusk from Knoxville on March 22, 1946. They have four children. Evelyn currently resides in Knoxville.

George David Swingle, II, was born on May 11, 1947. He married Jennifer Brown, and they have one daughter, Sarah, who was born in December of 1978.

Jane Lauren Swingle was born on November 11, 1953. She married Jeff Perry. (They are now divorced.) They have one son, Vincent Lee, who was born on January 15, 1986.

Susan Elaine Swingle was born on November 4, 1958. She married Steve Kimberlain.

Marjorie Anne Swingle was born on April 15, 1963. She married Mark VanDoren.

Interview with Margaret Ann Swingle on August 19, 1993
and telephone interview with Evelyn Swingle on August 5 and 9, 1993

GEORGE L. HATCHER, JR.
Service #14123158
POW #1757

When George Hatcher attended Sunday school and church at First Christian Church in Erwin on December 7, 1941, he had no idea what the events of that day would mean in his life.

While at church, he was informed by J. Floyd Meredith, the Road Foreman of Engineers for Clinchfield Railroad, to be in his office at eight o'clock the next morning to be hired as a locomotive fireman. After church, George walked down to Coley's Pharmacy, a soda fountain that was a popular hangout for the young people of Erwin. It was there that he heard the news about Pearl Harbor.

George L. Hatcher, Jr., was born in Erwin on October 14, 1920. His mother was Fanny Lasure Hatcher and his father was George L. Hatcher, Sr., a conductor on the Clinchfield Railroad.

There were eleven children in the Hatcher family: Thomas Edward (Ed), who married Virginia Moore; Lois Celeste, who died at age ten; George L., Jr., who married Virginia Bailey; Margie Joella, who married Jack Hawkins; Robert Wilson, who married Ethel Louise Smith; Virginia Dare (Norma), who married Jack Ingle; Betty Alice, who married Gene Frye; Wilma Jean, who married Joe Huskins; Philip David; Sue Ann, who married Travis Hughes; and Alvin Mason (Happy).

The Hatcher family lived in a large home in the Canah Chapel area. Mrs. Hatcher probably had trouble keeping track of her children because there were so many friends constantly in and out of the house, especially in the summertime. The Hatcher home was situated near North Indian Creek. The children dug out and dammed up a swimming hole, known as Hatcher's Hole. It was a very busy place all summer long.

Two of George's brothers also served during World War II. Ed was in the Air Corps, and Bob was in the Navy. George attended Love Street and Canah Chapel grade schools and graduated from Unicoi County High School with the class of 1940.

George worked at Unaka Stores after school and during the summer months. On December 8, 1941, he was hired as a fireman on the Clinchfield Railroad.

George enlisted in the Air Corps on June 25, 1942, after only six

George in uniform

months of work on the railroad. He had no formal leave of absence, but the Clinchfield Railroad let it be known that when any railroad employee left his job to serve his country, the job would still be there for him when he got home.

George had basic training at Keesler Field, Mississippi. From there he went to Sioux Falls, South Dakota, for seven and a half months of radio school and to learn code. He graduated and was promoted to buck sergeant. He then went to Las Vegas, Nevada, for six weeks of gunnery school and graduated as staff sergeant. From Las Vegas he was sent to Kearney, Nebraska, to be assigned as a crew member on a new B-17 G which the crew flew and tested for 100 hours in the states before heading overseas. The plane was given the name *Delayed Lady*.

THE CREW OF THE *DELAYED LADY*:
- Pilot - William Dee - Ft. Lauderdale, Florida - POW
- Co-pilot - Bob Cotterell - - Wounded - POW
- Navigator - Larry Oberstein - - Killed
- Bombardier - Donald S. Jay - Illinois - POW
- Engineer - William H. Jones - Bakersfield, California - POW
- Left Waist Gunner - Orvil Sterner - Los Angeles, California - POW
- Right Waist Gunner - Stephen Floyd - Camden, New Jersey - POW
- Ball Turret Gunner - Steve Sak - Chicago, Illinois - POW
- Tail Gunner - Tommy Treadwell - Arcadia, Florida - POW
- Radio Operator - George Hatcher - Erwin, Tennessee - POW

From the States, they went by way of Bangor, Maine; Iceland; Greenland; and Ireland to Peterborough, England. They were assigned to the 749th Bomb Squadron, 451st Bomb Group, of the 8th Air Corps.

After getting settled in at the base, George was able to get in touch with his brother Ed and got a pass to visit him in Manchester.

The first mission for the *Delayed Lady* was to bomb a submarine base at Kiel, Germany. The target for their second mission was oil refineries at Ludwigshafen, Germany. According to *Stars and Stripes,* there were 700 bombers on that mission on May 27, 1944. Two hundred and fifty ME-109 fighters came out of the sun to attack the bombers head on. George's plane was the second lead ship in formation. They were flying at 27,000 feet, loaded with eleven 500-pound bombs.

The first George knew of being under attack was when he heard

Crew of the *Delayed Lady* L-R: back row - Sterner, Hatcher, Floyd, Sak, Jones, and Treadwell; front row - Dee, Cotterell, Oberstein, and Jay.

machine-gun fire. Two of the four engines were shot out. The navigator was wounded with three 303s in his shoulder, and the co-pilot had a 20mm through his arm and in his leg.

The plane was forced to fall out of formation and salvo the eleven bombs that they were carrying. They were then attacked by eight or ten fighter planes which they were able to fight off. They changed course back to England, but had to fly over an artillery battery and were struck by two direct hits in the bomb bay and right wing, which set the right wing gasoline tank on fire.

The explosion turned the plane over and knocked George down. He was dazed but was able to put his parachute on. The bail-out bell rang. George went to the rear to bail out. The two waist gunners had already pulled the emergency release handle, and the door had been ejected. The gunners were standing in the doorway, looking out. They seemed to be frozen in place, and George couldn't get by. The flames were coming out of the gas tank on the right wing, and he was afraid the plane was ready to blow up. He backed up to the left side of the fuselage and ran as hard as he could toward the two men standing in the door. He took them out with him.

George and the two gunners opened their chutes at about the same time, and as they were coming down, George watched the others so he could get an idea of where they would land, hoping they could find each other. They seemed to be about a mile apart while in the air.

From the time the plane had taken off until they bailed out, things had been very noisy. As George was floating to the ground, he realized just how quiet it was. He was so high up that he had no sensation of falling. When he was in the plane, he had prayed to be saved; as he drifted toward the earth, he thanked God for delivering him from death.

The men had had no experience in bailing out. They were not instructed in parachute training except how to strap on the chute. They were instructed to tie their regular shoes to their parachute harness so they would have them when they landed. They took off their regular shoes when they got aboard the plane in order to put on the heated flight suits and boots. When George bailed out, he opened his chute too soon. The wash from the props quickly opened the chute with a jerk, breaking the ties on the shoes and causing them to be lost.

George looked toward the ground occasionally. It didn't seem to be getting any closer until he was almost down, then it seemed to come up fast. He landed on top of a small hill and intended to remove his parachute and look for his crew members. But as soon as he landed, he heard a voice he didn't understand, and several civilian men climbed out of a hole (probably a bomb crater).

They took him prisoner, searched him, and asked him if he had a pistol. He did not. He was pushed down the hill into the small town of Brebock. The street was paved with brick. As he was led down the street, the people on both sides of the street yelled at him. The only word he was able to make out was "swine." There was one man standing in the middle of the street, facing George. The guards held their prisoner on each side. The man tried to hit George with a haymaker, but he was able to duck.

The guards rushed him into a small building. Inside were some of his crew members. Larry Oberstein was unconscious. Some of the other crew members told George that Oberstein had been hit in the shoulder by by three 303s and was unconscious when the bail-out bell rang. He was put out of the plane on a cord that automatically opened his chute and was still unconscious when the Germans picked him up.

George said that Oberstein's throat was cut from ear to ear, and that he wanted to bandage it with one of the large bandages that came in the first-aid kit attached to their parachute packs. The guards knocked George down and made him to understand that he was not to help in any way. The crew members do not know if his throat was deliberately cut. They only saw his shoulder wound while on the plane. Oberstein had an "H," for Hebrew, on his dog tag—the Germans knew he was Jewish.

All the crew members were put on a flatbed truck and taken up a winding dirt road to the top of a mountain where there was an artillery battery. Most of the people there were young men, twelve to fifteen years old. They all wore khaki shorts and shirts.

They took pictures of George and the other prisoners. He thinks that these young men were the ones who shot them down.

From the top of the mountain, the men were taken to a jail where they stayed for a couple of days. Then they went to Dulag Luft, near Frankfurt, for interrogation.

George was given a form to fill out that was headed, in bold letters, "International Red Cross." The first line asked for name, rank, and serial

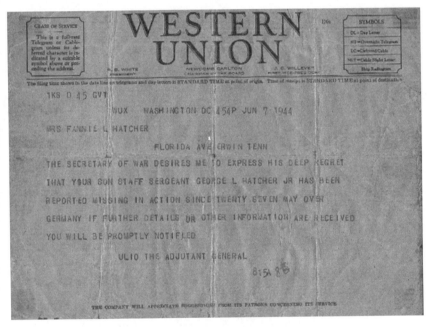

Telegram reporting George missing in action

number. The other lines asked for information about military training. George filled out the first line and handed the paper back. The interrogator laughed and said the information was for the Red Cross, and the sooner he filled it out, the sooner his parents would know he was alive. George refused to answer. The interrogator told him to answer the questions at the bottom of the page asking if his plane had been shot down by artillery or fighters. He again refused to answer. He was told to write "flack," and he again refused. The German said, "I am telling you to write 'flack'." George told him if he wanted it written, to write it himself. That finished the interrogation.

George was put on a train with four or five of his crew members. There was one guard, who carried a rifle slung around his neck. He also

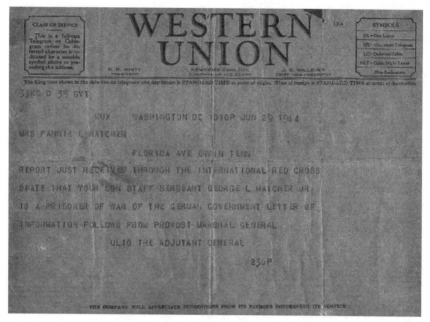

Telegram reporting George as prisoner

had a satchel with a strap. When it was time to eat, he opened the satchel and took out a loaf of black bread and some kind of jam in a quart jar. The guard cut one piece of bread for each prisoner and, with his knife, spread some "jerry-berry" jam on each piece.

The men were on the train for several days until they arrived at Stalag Luft IV. George's group was among the first hundred or so to be imprisoned at the camp, which had just been built. It had four lagers separated by a double fence about fifteen feet wide, with a warning rail about fifty feet from the fence. There were signs that read, "Anyone who touches fence will be shot at."

According to the Geneva Treaty, the airmen could not be forced to work. They had very little food, but plenty of cold water. When George first arrived at the camp, he received a Red Cross package containing one pair of English shoes, one shirt, one pair of pants, a razor, and blades.

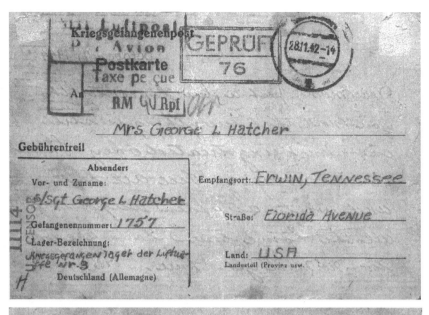

George sent home this card from prison camp in October 1944, signed "June," for "Junior."

This was all the clothing he received during the entire time he was there. The YMCA, through the Red Cross, sent balls, bats, cards, gloves, musical instruments, and other things that were life savers.

After being at Stalag Luft IV for a couple of months, the prisoners began getting a little more food, but it was awful. It was some kind of dehydrated vegetables that they called "green death." They would hold their breath and drink it, then catch their breath, and most of it would come back up. There were bugs and worms in the food. It was "Eat or starve." When George enlisted, he weighed 168 pounds. When liberated, he weighed 134 pounds.

During the time of imprisonment, on the marches, and at other times, George saw many dogs. They were all German shepherds. Apparently a guard dog was issued for every so many guards.

George received only three of the many post cards and letters from his family during the whole time he was a POW.

The Russian workers at the prison camp used oxen to pull the "honey wagon." The "honey wagon" was a large wooden tub on wheels. This apparatus was used to pump out the latrines. The waste was then taken outside the camp and dumped.

One occasion that George particularly remembers is when Carl Griffith, from Phoenix, Arizona, was clowning around and acted as if he were salting the tail of one of the oxen. He actually did take a bite. The ox jumped about two feet off the ground. Griffith and George were both rather happy-go-lucky and tried to keep up their own morale as well as that of the other prisoners.

Another memory of the camp is the time when John R. Hopp from Ft. Worth, Texas, wanted George to cut his hair with a razor blade. George said he was no barber, but Hopp insisted. So George cut his hair. It was a mess.

When the plane stopped in Iceland on the way overseas, George had bought a coonskin cap. When they got to Peterborough, George's crew was put into a quonset hut with another crew. One of the members of the crew had a new officer's blouse. George made a deal with him. If the other airman got shot down, George would get the officer's blouse; and if George got shot down, the other airman would get the coonskin cap. They shook hands on the deal. George said he could not remember the man's name. After he was in the prison camp, George said he thought, "Yeah, some guy is running around in England wearing my coonskin cap." After being in the prison camp for about two weeks, who should George see arrive but the airman who had won his cap.

Church services were conducted every Sunday while the men were in the prison camp.

When the Red Cross packages arrived at the camp, they contained all brands of American cigarettes. The men noticed that the packs of Old

Gold cigarettes had part of the back cut from each pack. This certainly was a puzzlement. After liberation, the first chance that George had to see a pack of Old Gold cigarettes, he looked at the back and found the words "Freedom is our Heritage." These words had been cut from all the packs that had been delivered to the camp.

The prisoners in Stalag Luft IV were occasionally allowed outside to gather vegetation, weeds, grass, hay, or whatever they could find to fill their mattresses. George said they found an abundance of chaff all over the area where they were raking. Chaff was metallic strands, very similar to the silver icicles used to decorate Christmas trees. This chaff was carried on the bombers and released into the air through a chute near the radio. The motors of the plane dispersed it in the area of the bombers. The chaff was used to distort the enemy radar.

As the war was winding down, the prisoners were taken from Stalag Luft IV to Stalag Luft XIII B, near Nuremberg, Germany. George and Allen Alford were in the first group to leave Stalag Luft IV. They were marched from the camp for about three fourths of a mile and put into 40×8 boxcars. These were the boxcars that were made to hold forty men or eight horses. Many more than forty men were jammed into the boxcar. They took turns standing or sitting and were in the boxcars for several days before arriving at Stalag Luft XIII B.

The RAF was still bombing by night, and the Americans by day. The Germans had artillery all around the camp. Guns and sirens went off constantly. The buildings were made of wood, so the prisoners used tin cans and boards from the buildings to dig trenches to protect themselves from the shrapnel. They were at Stalag Luft XIII B for about six weeks.

When General Patton broke across the Rhine River, the prisoners were marched out of the camp about dawn one morning. After they had marched for two or three hours, the area was strafed by American P-47s. George said they were actually shooting at a train that was very close to the marchers. The prisoners were marching five abreast. When the strafing started, George and a man named Kasper (from Pennsylvania) ran for cover in a forest of pine trees. It was a terrifying experience.

There were about 15,000 American Air Corps NCOs and two American colonels in the group of marchers. They had one Luftwaffe captain, Captain Wolf, and several German soldiers as guards. Some of the guards were walking, and some were on bicycles. After the brush with the P-47s, the prisoners gathered what white clothing they had and spelled out AAF-POW. As the P-47s continued to pass over, they dipped their wings to the POWs.

On the first or second day after leaving Nuremberg, the prisoners received word of the death of President Roosevelt. Someone went up on a hill and played taps while all the prisoners stood at attention. They then continued the march.

While in the prison camp, George tried to keep physically fit as best he could. Even though half starved, he exercised every day by walking, running, or jogging around the lager. Steve Floyd, one of the crew members from the *Delayed Lady*, was in a different building, and George tried to get him to exercise with him. But Floyd would not, saying that he was saving his shoes, which he did. After a year in the camp, Floyd's shoes were not even broken in. George felt that when they got out of the prison camp, they would have to do a lot of walking, and he wanted to be in shape to do so and to have his shoes broken in.

After the first day of the march from Nuremberg, Floyd called George to look at his feet. They were a mass of blisters. Someone had a sewing kit with a needle. George used the needle to drain the water from the blisters, and he told Floyd to put his socks and shoes back on and lace them as tight as possible, because they had to go on. Floyd just sat and cried. Several of the men half carried and urged him to start walking, but he wouldn't. After a time, all the men had marched ahead, and only Floyd and George were left. George got angry and told Floyd that he was going on without him. Floyd finally started walking. They barely made it across the Danube River before the Germans blew the bridge. After crossing, they met up with their group which had stopped to rest just around a bend from the river.

General Patton's 3rd Army was coming up behind the prisoners. When it got dark, the prisoners were marched into some woods and told to rest. The two American colonels passed the word for the prisoners to take as much time as possible when they were instructed to move. They were hoping to be overtaken by the American Army. When the prisoners were told to "roust," they stood up as if getting ready to move. But as the guards went on to wake up the next bunch, the prisoners would lie back down. When the guards would come back to "roust" them again, the other group would lie back down. This continued until well after sunup. The guards started shooting into the air and yelling for the men to move. The American Army was getting louder and closer. Finally, all the guards ran off. Captain Wolf called the prisoners together and said that they were free to go. He said he couldn't handle them, but if they would stay with him, he would protect them from the SS troops. Captain Wolf told them that it would only be a "fortnight" until he would be their prisoner.

Almost all the prisoners stayed with the captain, rather than trying to get through enemy lines to the Americans. They walked up a mountain, and when they reached the top, they rested for three days at a big farm where they slept in the barn.

The American people had heard about how Hitler had tried to put down all types of religion. On the march, George was surprised to see large crucifixes, some as tall as fifteen feet, in front of the farmhouses. The farm on the mountain where they stayed for three days was owned by a very religious family. The family did no work on Saturday, which was their Sabbath. The family allowed the prisoners to come in and use their kitchen to boil potatoes.

George says that the walking was the best part of his experience as a POW. The Red Cross was with them for most of the journey. They handled the Red Cross food parcels and unloaded them where the prisoners were going to spend the night. Then the Red Cross people went back to the rear and picked up the sick, wounded, and crippled, and took them to the place designated for rest. After that, the Red Cross people went back for more parcels. The trucks were white with red crosses on the sides and top. The prisoners called them "White Angels."

When the prisoners arrived at Moosburg, they were put in tents about 200 feet long in a large POW camp. By this time, everything was quiet—they hadn't heard the big guns for several days.

George heard a plane that sounded different, so he stuck his head out of the tent and saw a small Piper Cub with the biggest white star he had ever seen. He yelled for the other guys to come and look. At about the same time, they began to hear small arms fire.

The American tanks were coming around the hill. The guards in the towers were holding up their hands and shouting, "Comey Rod." They were shouting loudly enough to be heard in the next county. *Stars and Stripes* later reported that there were 127,000 Allied POWs liberated that day, April 29, 1945, at Moosburg, Germany. They were liberated by the 14th Armored Division of the 3rd Army.

The men had been told to stay in camp, but when the tanks came in and tore down the fences, George decided to take off for the town about a mile and a half away. The streets of Moosburg were made of brick. George was standing beside the street as the American tanks rolled by. He yelled and asked if they had any food. Someone tossed him a can of beans and franks.

The can rolled down an incline beside the road. George and two Russians ran for it; George won. After eating the beans and franks, he noticed that the POWs who had gathered along the street were yelling to tank crews and asking where they were from. When he yelled at the first tank, he asked if anyone was from Tennessee. The guy with his head out of the turret said, "Yes, where are you from?"

George replied, "From near Johnson City," thinking no one had heard of Erwin. Another fellow stuck his head out of the turret and said, "I'm from Erwin." As it turned out, he was Buster Wilson, whom George had known when Buster drove the truck and delivered groceries for A. R. Brown's store.

From Moosburg, George's group was flown to Camp Lucky Strike near Le Havre, France. At Camp Lucky Strike, they saw their pilot for the first time since being shot down. They hardly recognized him because he had lost so much weight. His ankle had been injured when he landed. He was not captured for ten days. When he was taken, he was accused of being a spy and was tortured by the SS.

In Le Havre, George boarded a liberty ship which stayed in port for two days before heading home. The crossing took about five days.

When he arrived in New York, George called home. That was the first news that his family had received about his being liberated.

George came home on leave for sixty-three days. He married Virginia Bailey on August 3, 1945. Virginia is the daughter of Bernie and Pearl Tipton Bailey.

After the sixty-three-day leave, George went to Miami Beach for the six weeks of rest and relaxation leave. He then went to Smyrna Air Base near Nashville, Tennessee, and later to Maxwell Field, Alabama, for discharge on October 20, 1945.

After the war, all the men from George's crew were able to get in touch with each other, except Orville Sterner. They knew he had been a POW, and George had seen him at Camp Lucky Strike, but they completely lost track of him when the war was over.

Larry Oberstein's mother called George when he was on leave after he first arrived home. She asked for details of her son's death. George said he just couldn't bring himself to tell her what happened. He told her he would get in touch with her later, but he never did. George can't remember where Oberstein was from. Larry Oberstein was the only crew member to be killed.

George went back to work for the railroad on October 22, 1945. He said he couldn't wait to get back to work. The railroad has been good to George. He and his brother Ed had the honor of running the little #1 engine. About 1965, a small steam engine that had been stored in Erwin for years was refurbished and put into operation. It was used to pull excursion trains along the Clinchfield line, especially through the Nolichucky gorge in the fall when they ran the "Autumn Leaf Special." The engine was referred to as "Clinchfield #1."

George and Ed got the job of running the little engine because they were two of the few railroad men who were capable of running a steam

George on Clinchfield #1 engine

locomotive. The other knowledgeable men were much older and not physically able to do the job. Ed was the engineer and George, the fire-man. They seemed to be carrying on a family tradition. Their father and grandfather had worked for the Clinchfield Railroad.

On one trip to St. Paul, Virginia (about 210 miles round-trip), using steam only and the Clinchfield #1 pulling several coaches, they filled the tender with coal in Erwin. The tender held eight and a half tons. They filled it again in Johnson City and again in Kingsport. In St. Paul they filled it again for the return trip as well as in Kingsport and Johnson City on the way back. At six o'clock that morning, George had weighed him-self before going to work. When he got home that night, he weighed again. He had lost twelve pounds from shoveling all that coal.

On the excursion runs, the little #1 engine was in front for looks, but a diesel would be behind doing the heavy work. The little steam locomo-

Ed and George Hatcher stand beside Clinchfield #1 engine.

George and Ed stand in front of Clinchfield # 1 engine.

George Hatcher, P.O. Likens, and Ed Hatcher

tive had to be kept fired at all times because of the mechanics of the engine.

When not running the little engine, Ed had a regular run on a freight train to Spartanburg, South Carolina. George had the pusher run. He worked on the diesels that pushed the trains over the Blue Ridge.

The little Clinchfield #1 stayed in operation for approximately thirteen years. During that time George and Ed made many runs on the train. At one time they toured Florida for fifteen days. They carried Howard Baker on two campaign trips, and the Clinchfield #1 was used for "The Santa Claus Special" during its years of service.

During a stop on one of the excursion runs, Ed told George to come back to the coach to meet General Moore. George and General Moore started talking about being in World War II. The General said he had been the commanding officer when the prisoners were liberated at Moosburg. George said, "You mean you were the Commanding Officer of the 14th Armored Division of the 3rd Army?" General Moore was surprised that George remembered exactly which outfit liberated him.

George certainly keeps up his physical condition. He has been running in competition for about twenty years. He ran in the local "Apple Festival" races three times. One year he came in first in the 5K race. Another year he came in second in the 10K race, and another year he came in third in the 10K race. He came in first in the 5K Blueberry Road Race in Alma, Georgia, and has won several trophies for being the oldest

The Hatcher grandchildren, L-R: Michael Callahan, Shannon Briggs, Julie Briggs, Jodi Rohling, and Alan Callahan in February 1983.

The Hatcher family: Brenda Rudman, Virginia Hatcher, Linda Rohling, George Hatcher and Beth Briggs.

George shows off one of his fishing trophies.

runner.

George and Virginia have three daughters.

Mary Beth married Larry Briggs. They have a son, Shannon, and a daughter, Julie. They live in Erwin.

The twin daughters are Brenda Sue and Linda Lou. Brenda married (1) Tommy Warrick and (2) Mel Rudman. They have no children. They reside in Palm Desert, California.

Linda married (1) Bill Callahan. They have two sons, Alan and Michael. She married (2) Tom Rohling. They have a daughter, Jodi, and live in Oak Ridge, Tennessee.

George likes to fish and has had a houseboat at Watauga Lake. He can often be found at the Clinchfield Drug Store, swapping stories with the other retired railroaders who hang out there.

George keeps in shape by jogging on the Erwin Bypass on January 31, 1980.

Interview with George Hatcher, Jr., taped in July 1992

JOSEPH FREDRICK MILLER
Service #14162032
POW #6422

J. Fred Miller was born in Erwin on January 18, 1924, making him just under nineteen years old when he enlisted. He attended Love Street and Love Chapel Schools during his grade school years, then Unicoi County High School.

Fred didn't wait to graduate from high school with the class of 1943. Instead, he joined the U.S. Army Air Corps on December 12, 1942. He had waited until football season was over during his senior year because he was on the team.

He remembers growing up in Erwin with an ideal childhood. Even though the country was in midst of the depression, Fred doesn't remember that any of his acquaintances were deprived. There was always something to eat, something to do, and somewhere to go (either on foot or by bicycle).

Fred's family consisted of his parents, Hyder and Lena Belcher Miller, three brothers, and three sisters. Both of his parents worked at Southern Potteries, Inc. His grandparents were Joseph and Ellen Robinson Belcher from Virginia, and William and Teupa Bennett Miller from Poplar, North Carolina.

Two of Fred's brothers also served during World War II—Clarence in the Navy, and Hubert in the Army. His youngest brother, James, spent two years in the Army after graduating from Clemson.

His sister Mildred is married to Roy Silvers, Wilma Ann is married to Ben Childers, and Brenda is married to Robert Kegley.

When talking about growing up in Erwin, Fred said he had recently watched something on TV about the gangster era, and it brought back memories of how he used to listen to stories of Al Capone, John Dillinger, and Baby Face Nelson. Those stood out as fascinating stories to a ten- or twelve-year-old boy.

On weekends, Fred worked at a local grocery store. He remembers going to the movies on Saturdays for a dime. It was a happy time!

Fred's grandson Jason, who lives in South Dakota, visited Erwin in 1991. Fred took him all over the county, including out to Love Station to see the old home place. They parked and Fred told Jason how it was

Joseph Fredrick Miller

growing up there during the '30s. He said that his grandson just grinned and said, "But Papaw, what did you DO?" Fred told him, "We LIVED and enjoyed life!"

After enlisting on December 12, 1942, Fred was sent to Ft. Oglethorpe, Georgia. Right away his training was delayed, because ten days after enlisting, he had to undergo an appendectomy. After a thirty-day delay, he was sent to Miami Beach for basic training, then to Gulfport, Mississippi; Loredo, Texas; and Ypsilanti, Michigan. Fred's group then went to Salt Lake City, Utah, where the crews were made up. From there his crew took a train to Wichita, Kansas, to pick up its own plane. This was something new. They test flew the plane four or five times to be sure it checked out okay, and then flew it to Colorado Springs, Colorado, for combat training. (The plane was built in Ypsilanti, Michigan, and assembled in Wichita, Kansas.)

While in Colorado Springs, Fred sent for his fiancée, Sue Sams. They were married in the base chapel on January 24, 1944. From Colorado Springs the crew flew to Homestead Army Air Corps Base in Florida to be checked out, get all the necessary shots, etc.

Fred and Sue

Fred

The *Emperor Jones* and crew went overseas to Cerignola, Italy, in April of 1944. The plane was a B-24 of the 744 Bomb Squadron, 456th Bomb Group, of the 15th Air Corps. They were the only crew ever to fly the plane. Fred thinks it was something new to have the same crew and plane for all missions. Perhaps it was to make the crew feel closer, work better together, and accomplish more missions. Whatever the reason, it worked very well because the *Emperor Jones* completed thirty-four missions.

Planes flying out of England were required to fly only twenty-five missions, whereas those flying out of Italy required fifty missions.

While stationed at Cerignola, a small village in the heel of the Italian boot, the crews were put up in tents instead of regular barracks. The weather was warm, but there was a lot of rain. The crew went into the small village only a few times. There wasn't much to see or do. The way they were working and flying, they didn't have time for anything except to plop into bed as soon as they retuned from a mission, then get up and start all over again. Fred did get to Foggia, about thirty miles away, once while he was there.

The name *Emperor Jones* was chosen in "honor" of their pilot, 1st Lieutenant Edward C. Jones of Memphis, Tennessee. He was twenty-four years old and had been flying since he was fourteen. Jones had been a cotton crop duster and was well respected as a pilot, even though the men did not particularly like him as a man. They said he acted like an emperor. Jones actually got a kick out of why they named the plane as they did.

Fred said Jones was such a good pilot that he pulled them out of many hairy situations. One time was when they were on their way overseas. They ran into a tropical storm in South America. Fred remembered the plane was tossed around so much that he felt the wings would come off. He said Jones pulled them through the storm with the most amazing expertise imaginable.

Jones, who constantly pushed the crew, was working for captain's bars. The *Emperor Jones* flew more missions without rest than required. At one time they flew for thirteen days straight. They were supposed to have a rest period after twenty-five missions, but they didn't.

The crew was on the verge of collapsing when they began their thirty-fifth mission. Jones told the crew that after this mission, they could fly the plane to Cairo for a two-week rest leave.

Vittorio Orlando Emanuel Domenick Russo was the co-pilot. (Fred always remembered all the names.) Russo, who was from Newark, New Jersey, was called "Vic" by all the crew. He was well liked. They got along very well with him, especially the few times they got away from the base, because he spoke Italian fluently. Russo became a POW.

Benjamin Grant, the navigator, was from Albany, New York. He was fresh out of navigation school and became a POW.

Joseph Woll, the bombardier, was a very good friend of Fred's. He was a farmer from Summit Station, Pennsylvania. Fred said Joe was the most tenderhearted man he had ever known. After a bombing run, the other fellows would kid Joe and ask him how many civilians he had killed that day. Joe would just sit and cry. Joseph Woll was killed.

James Sanford, the tail gunner, was from East Quorque, New Jersey. He had flown more than fifty missions in the South Pacific, been home on leave, then sent overseas again on the *Emperor Jones*. Sanford was killed.

Walter J. Rogers, the ball turret (belly) gunner, was from Bessemer, Alabama. He was a special friend of Fred's. While they were in Colorado Springs, Walter (called Jay), his wife, Phyllis, and Fred and Sue shared an apartment. Walter J. Rogers was killed.

Ferrell E. Daniel, the top turret gunner, was from Knoxville, Tennessee. He was a very quiet person. He became a POW.

Jack F. Bonifield, the radioman and left waist gunner, was from Delhi, Oklahoma. He was not a regular crew member, having replaced Ralph Zetterberg from Long Island, New York, who was in the hospital with wounds from a previous mission. Bonifield became a POW.

Harold E. Rogers, the nose gunner, was from Hollywood, California. He was six feet tall and had been a stunt man in the movies. He had doubled for Cary Grant, John Wayne, and others. Rogers was killed.

Joseph M. Michaud from Chicopee Falls, Massachusetts, was not a crew member. He was a photographer for the squadron and went along on bombing raids. He could go up in any plane he wanted to, but he always chose the *Emperor Jones* because he knew and liked the crew so well. Michaud became a POW.

Fred served as the engineer for the *Emperor Jones*.

The appendix lists the rank, duty station, next of kin, and address of each crew member at time of enlistment.

Seven bombers left Cerignola, Italy, on July 2, 1944. Their targets were the oil fields of Budapest, Hungary. They made their bomb drops, apparently on target, because the smoke was so thick. They were flying at 22,000 feet and flack was very heavy. Several of the bombers had been hit and had dropped out of formation. As the *Emperor Jones* circled back over the target to return to Italy, they were attacked by a group of German FW-190 and ME-109 fighters, which were flying six or seven abreast. The *Emperor Jones* was immediately hit.

Crew of the *Emperor Jones*, L-R: standing - Woll, Jones, Russo, and Grant; kneeling - Miller, Harold Rogers, Sanford, Daniel, and Jay Rogers.

Of the seven bombers that left Cerignola that day, only one returned. Ironically, Fred had a friend waiting for the mission to return. Tom Hensley, from Erwin, was stationed at Bari, Italy, with the Headquarters Company of the 484th Bomb Group, 15th Air Corps. Tom had heard from home that Fred was in Cerignola, so he was there waiting for a plane that did not return.

After being hit, the plane was burning so badly that all communications were out. As the crew was getting ready to bail out, a 20mm shell from one of the fighter planes came inside the plane and took off a kneecap from Michaud, who was sitting on the escape hatch still taking pictures. Two pieces of the shell hit Bonifield in the back, and pieces hit Fred in the left leg.

Fred was able to pull Bonifield over to where Michaud was sitting. They had chest-type parachutes which they had to put on. Fred helped Michaud get his chute on, then opened the escape hatch door, and pushed him out. He then put the chute on Bonifield, who was practically helpless, and rolled him out the door. The fire was so intense toward the back of the plane that there was no way Fred could get to Sanford, the tail gunner. He knew that Rogers was already dead because of the way the ball turret was shot up. By this time, Fred's oxygen mask was on fire, and he had to take it off. Then he jumped. The men who got out saw the plane blow up.

Later, Fred and Ferrell Daniel were recounting what else happened. Daniel told Fred that Russo, Grant, and he bailed out of the bomb bay and upper part of the plane. Daniel said Jones had stood up, as if to bail out, then just gave a negative shake of his head and sat back down and didn't attempt to get out. No one knows why. When Grant jumped out, Woll was standing right behind him, but the plane blew up before Woll could get out.

Bonifield had two pieces of the shell in his back and spent two months in a German hospital before being taken to a POW camp. Fred still keeps in touch with Bonifield, who is now retired after working as a mail carrier in Sayre, Oklahoma. Fred was in touch with Michaud for a while after the war. Michaud had a permanent limp as a result of his injury.

The plane was at about 20,000 feet when Fred jumped, and he figured he was about twenty miles from Budapest. As he was drifting to the ground, he could see a barbed wire fence winding through the middle of what appeared to be an alfalfa field. He said his only thoughts were that he was going to land astraddle that fence! He managed to maneuver, cross his legs, and land about five feet from the wire. He bundled up his parachute and started walking across the field.

A group of Hungarian peasants immediately began to surround him. They were carrying hoe handles, picks, and shovels. They all seemed to be talking at once, and Fred couldn't understand a word. He did, however, make out the word "pistola." He indicated to them that he did not have a pistol. About that time, someone hit him on the head with a hoe handle, knocking him to the ground. He got back up, and it seemed that everyone with a weapon began beating him. Fred already had serious burns on his face from the oxygen mask fire, as well as wounds on his left leg. He feels that he would have been beaten to death if two Hungarian soldiers on motorcycles had not come by at that time. The soldiers stopped the beating, put Fred on the back of one of the motorcycles, and took him into Budapest to the military headquarters that in peacetime had been a prison. Even though he was in very bad condition, he received no medical attention.

At the military headquarters, Fred was interrogated by a very fat Hungarian who spoke perfect English. The fat Hungarian explained to Fred just why the Hungarian people hated the American flyers so much. The

WESTERN UNION 1204

CLASS OF SERVICE
This is a full-rate Telegram or Cablegram unless its deferred character is indicated by a suitable symbol above or preceding the address.

R. B. WHITE
PRESIDENT

NEWCOMB CARLTON
CHAIRMAN OF THE BOARD

J. C. WILLEVER
FIRST VICE-PRESIDENT

The filing time shown in the date line on telegrams and day letters is STANDARD TIME at point of origin. Time of receipt is STANDARD

22KS D 43 GVT WUX

WASHINGTON DC 1040A JUL 14 1944

MRS SUE E MILLER

238 CATAWBA ST ERWIN TENN

THE SECRETARY OF WAR DESIRES ME TO EXPRESS HIS DEEP
REGRET THAT YOUR HUSBAND STAFF SERGEANT JOSEPH F MILLER
HAS BEEN REPORTED MISSING IN ACTION SINCE TWO JULY
OVER HUNGARY IF FURTHER DETAILS OR OTHER INFORMATION
ARE RECEIVED YOU WILL BE PROMPTLY NOTIFIED

ULIO THE ADJUTANT GENERAL

WESTERN UNION 1204

CLASS OF SERVICE
This is a full-rate Telegram or Cablegram unless its deferred character is indicated by a suitable symbol above or preceding the address.

A. N. WILLIAMS
PRESIDENT

NEWCOMB CARLTON
CHAIRMAN OF THE BOARD

J. C. WILLEVER
FIRST VICE-PRESIDENT

The filing time shown in the date line on telegrams and day letters is STANDARD TIME at point of origin. Time of receipt is STANDARD

2KS D 34 GVT

WUX WASHINGTON DC 946P SEP 10 1944

MRS SUE E MILLER

238 CATAWBA ST ERWIN TENN

REPORT JUST RECEIVED THROUGH THE INTERNATIONAL RED CROSS
STATES THAT YOUR HUSBAND STAFF SERGEANT JOSEPH F MILLER
IS A PRISONER OF WAR OF THE GERMAN GOVERNMENT LETTER OF
INFORMATION FOLLOWS FROM PROVOST MARSHAL GENERAL

J A ULIO THE ADJUTANT GENERAL

820A

Western Union telegrams report Fred as missing and then as a POW.

Hungarians had been told, as part of Hitler's propaganda program, that the American flyers were dropping booby-trapped dolls and children's toys, and that Hungarian children were being killed by American flyers in this way. No wonder the peasants were ready to kill any American flyer within reach.

Fred was put into a cell in the lower part of the prison that he called the dungeon. It had no windows—just a small opening in the door where the guard could look in. Each morning, for twenty-two days, he was taken from the cell, led upstairs, and interrogated. He could only tell them the same thing each day—that he was a U. S. flyer and knew no military secrets. He was then taken outside, made to stand against a rock wall, blindfolded, and left standing there for an hour or more, not knowing whether or not he would be shot. During this time, he received no medical care whatsoever, and he was a nervous wreck from the extreme tension and pain. At the end of twenty-two days, German soldiers came in and took him to Stalag Luft IV.

Fred still has nightmares about the filth and unsanitary conditions he experienced during the trip to Stalag Luft IV. Fifty-three prisoners were crammed into a "40×8" boxcar that was smaller than American boxcars. The floor was covered with straw. The prisoners were in the boxcar for six days and six nights without being let outside. All the prisoners could not sit down at one time. If one stood up, he lost his sitting space. Once a day the prisoners were given two German sausages (about the size of two large rolls of bologna) to be divided among the fifty-three men. They were brought a five-gallon bucket of water for drinking. When the water was gone, the bucket was used for a toilet facility. The bucket was then taken out and returned full of drinking water.

One of the nights, about midnight, during his six-day and six-night nightmare trip, the boxcar was parked in the rail yards in Vienna, Austria, when the British were bombing. The bombs fell so close that the boxcar rocked back and forth.

The prisoners arrived about a mile from Stalag Luft IV and were taken by truck on to the camp. As Fred was going through the gate, he heard someone yell, "Hey, Miller, what the hell are you doing here?" It was Clyde Tinker. Clyde recognized Fred; but Jim Hensley, who was also there, did not, because by this time Fred was very skinny and had many bad scabs on his face from the wounds and burns.

Prisoners were brought in almost everyday, and it became a habit for the old prisoners to watch as the new men came in to see if they knew any of them.

Ferrell Daniel, of Knoxville, was the only one of Fred's crew members in the prison camp with him. It wasn't until after the war that Fred was able to learn the fate of the other crew members.

The German guards and German administration began to wonder about the small town of Erwin. The fact that Erwin was a common German name, and since at that time Erwin Rommel was a hero to the German people, the name obviously made an impression. When more than three or four men from Erwin showed up in the camp, no doubt they were puzzled. Even more of a puzzlement was when they learned that these men all knew each other personally.

Most of the German guards of Fred's section were fairly decent people. They were especially fond of the soap and chocolate (called D bars) that the prisoners received in their Red Cross food packages. The prisoners traded the chocolate and soap for light bulbs, electric wire, coils, and other things that the guards smuggled in. With these, the men built a short-wave radio and kept track of what was happening as Patton marched across Germany. When Roosevelt died, the Germans tried to tell the prisoners that he had committed suicide, but the men knew better because they were able to listen to the BBC on the radio.

Each prisoner was supposed to receive a Red Cross package once a week. In the beginning of Fred's confinement, they received packages, but they had to be shared by three or four persons. The packages dwindled down as the war went on. The prisoners felt that the Germans were keeping them for themselves. Occasionally a deck of cards came through in a Red Cross package, and the men had something to do to relieve the boredom.

In February of 1945, when the Americans, British, and Russians were closing in on Stalag Luft IV, the camp was deserted, and the prisoners were sent to other camps. Fred was put on a train and was separated from the other Erwin men who went on the march. This trip in the boxcar lasted for six days but wasn't as bad as the trip from Budapest to Stalag Luft IV. This time he was taken to Stalag Luft I, near Barth, Germany, very close to the Swedish border. He remained there until May 1, when they were liberated by the Russians.

At Stalag Luft I, there were several black prisoners who had come from Ramitelli in Italy. Fred heard a story of how they had told the German guards that they were "night fighters." They said they had been injected with a secret serum that turned their skin black. They were believed!

Fred's bomber group had often been escorted on missions by P-47s

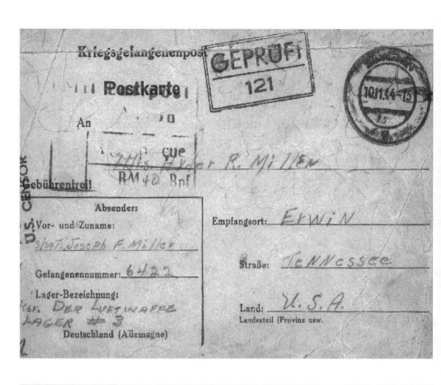

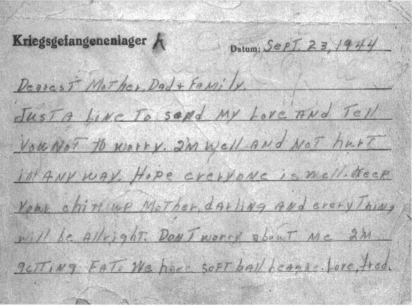

Fred sent this postcard to his family in September 1944.

that came from a black squadron stationed in Italy. After the interview with Fred, information was asked for and received about the black squadron. Lieutenant Colonel Alexander Jefferson, USAF, retired, of Detroit, Michigan, supplied the following information:

The black airmen came from the 99th, 100th, 301st, and 302nd Squadrons of the 332nd Fighter Group of the 15th Air Corps, based at Ramitelli, Italy. The fighter planes were called "Red Tails" because of the red markings on the tails of the planes.

Almost forty black airmen were POWs. When the war ended, they were at Stalag Luft VII A and Stalag Luft I.

Lieutenant Colonel Jefferson was a POW for nine months at Stalag Luft III and Stalag Luft VII A. He was one of the "Tuskegee Airmen," the first black pilots trained for the US Army Air Corps.

As the Russians closed in on Stalag Luft I, the Germans deserted the camp. The prisoners were there for twenty-four hours with no guards. Colonel Zempke, a P-47 pilot who had been shot down, was the highest ranking American in the camp, so he was in charge. Military routine, chain of command, and usual military procedures were followed. The colonel sent out scouts to contact the Americans, British, or Russians. After twenty-four hours, the Russians came in. That was a sight to behold—fifteen- and sixteen-year-old kids driving those big tanks and pushing down the barbed wire and fences. It was also sad, because the majority of those kids were drunk. They were well supplied with vodka.

The Russians kept the prisoners in the camp for about two weeks before they let the Americans come in to move them out. The Russians told the prisoners to wear white arm bands so they would not be mistaken for Germans.

The prisoners began to get more food, but they just couldn't take it. Their stomachs had shrunk so much that they could only eat small amounts. When the men were given meat, it was too rich to eat without making them sick.

Even though the Russians were in charge for about two weeks, the Americans were free to go as they pleased as long as they wore the white arm bands. They went into the town of Barth, which was about two miles from the camp. There was nothing there because the Russians had already leveled the town, but it was something to do. At least the men were free to go where they wanted.

About the fifteenth of May, the Americans came in and began to move the prisoners out. They were flown to Camp Lucky Strike, near Le

Havre, France.

They were at Camp Lucky Strike for about thirty days. While there, the men were given physical exams. The doctors told them that they would slowly have to force themselves to eat more food in order to stretch their stomachs back to normal. Fred normally weighed 170 pounds. When he got out of the prison camp, he weighed 110 pounds.

Also at Camp Lucky Strike, the men were allowed to go to Paris on leave. Fred took advantage of a three-day pass. He liked it so well, he took another three days AWOL. After the six days in Paris, he got back to the camp about 6:00 p.m. He lay down on his bunk, and then about 8:00 p.m. his sergeant came in and told him to get his clothes together because they were ready to load the boat.

The ship was an Italian liner that had been converted for carrying troops. They were at sea for seven days. Fred said, "You should have heard the noise that those POWs made when they sailed into New York Harbor and got their first glimpse of the Statue of Liberty!"

The POWs were taken to an Army base in New Jersey, probably Fort Dix, to be processed and have physicals, etc. They were there for eight or ten days. Then it was home to Erwin.

After the sixty-day leave in Erwin, Fred and Sue went to Miami Beach for two weeks. Then Fred went to Greenville, South Carolina, for a short time, then to Seymour Johnson Air Base in Goldsboro, North Carolina, for discharge on October 20, 1945.

After getting back home in October, Fred went to work for the Consolidated Feldspar Corporation in December 1945. He then went to the Feldspar Corporation in Spruce Pine, North Carolina, in 1949. From there, he returned to Consolidated Feldspar Corporation in February 1952, and was transferred to Denver, Colorado. In October 1959 the Miller family was transferred to Custer, South Dakota, where they lived until Fred retired in 1986, and they moved back home to Erwin.

The Millers have two children. Their daughter, Judi (Judith Lynn Culberson), has two sons, Matthew who is twenty-four years old and Jason who is twenty. They live in Pierre, South Dakota, where Judi is a science teacher.

The Millers' son, Joe (Joseph Fred Miller, II), lives in Birmingham, Alabama, where he is a shop foreman for a heavy equipment company. Joe married Rebecca Wellman. They have two sons, Jesse who is eleven years old and Jared who is seven.

Fred and Sue are enjoying their retirement years. They belong to Calvary Baptist Church, where Fred was a member before his Air Corps

Fred receives POW medal from Gen. Norman C. Gaddis on April 10, 1989.

Miller reunion in 1991, L-R: back row - Judi, Jason, Sue, Joe, and Becky; front row - Jared, Fred, and Jesse.

Jesse, Sue, Fred, and Jared during Christmas 1990 in Birmingham

service.

Sue has taken up the hobby of quilt making and has some gorgeous examples of her work. Fred plays golf, "putters" around the house, and enjoys the times when he gets together with the other Erwin POWs.

Interview with Fred Miller taped on August 25, 1991

Fred Miller died on July 11, 1992, at the VA Hospital in Johnson City, Tennessee.

P.O.W. Prayer

Oh God, we are in a strange land
    and among strange men,
And we wondered just when
    hostilities would end.
We lived with it, woke with it,
    and would we die?
No one at home understood this
    and why.

Alone—always lonely, and
    filled with harm
Understood only by a
    comrade-in-arms.
Love of your God, your country,
    and your own,
We never lost faith in our
    loved ones at home.

Our faith in God was our
    strongest might
As each of us would say to Him
    in our prayers every night—
"Help us, Oh Lord, to live for Thee.
    Because of our faith,
    someday we'll be free."

—Fred Miller

DICK LEE FRANKLIN
Service #14061861
POW #6520

Picture this—Johnson City, Tennessee—September 3, 1941—the corner of Main and Roan Streets—two young high school boys toss a coin to determine which they will join, the Army or the Navy. Dick Franklin won the toss, so the Army won out. That coin toss decided Dick's future for the next few years.

Let us go back a bit. Dick had attended high school for three years. He didn't learn much, but had a lot of fun. He played in the band and laid out of school frequently to go hunting and fishing.

Dick had worked during the summer of 1941 as a carpenter's helper, building a house on the upper end of New Street. Before school started in September, Dick's father asked him what he planned on doing. Dick said the draft had started and war seemed imminent, and thinking to get sympathy from his father, he told him he was thinking about joining the Army. He was really taken aback when his father agreed that was a great idea—seeing that he wasn't really interested in school.

When Dick went up to the high school to clean out his locker, he ran into Bill Britton who was on his way to band practice. Bill asked him what he was doing, and Dick told him he was on his way to join the Army. Bill said, "Wait a minute, I'll clean out my locker and go with you."

Dick and Bill played the only two baritone horns in the high school band. The band director was Wilkse Bobbitt. Dick wondered if he had a big problem with the fact that both of his baritone horn players left at the same time.

The next day, Dick and Bill hitchhiked to Johnson City and argued all the way. Bill had decided to join the Navy, but Dick still held out for the Army. So there on the corner they decided to toss a coin to see which branch of service they would join. The Army won.

The boys went to the Army Recruiting Office in the post office building. They informed the recruiter that they wanted to join "The Horse Cavalry in Fort Riley, Kansas." At that time there was a U. S. Army Cavalry. After a short exam, the recruiter sat down to talk seriously to the boys. He told them that the up and coming branch of the Army was the

Dick Lee Franklin

Air Corps and advised them that was the one in which to enlist. They did. Dick lied about his age; he was seventeen years and two days old.

Dick's family background is similar to most of the local people. His parents were Harry and Beth Tabb Franklin. His father and grandfather worked on the CC&O (or Clinchfield) Railroad. His paternal grandparents, Aaron and Emma Weld Franklin, had moved to Erwin in the early 1900s from North Carolina. His maternal grandparents, Henry and Nancy Elizabeth Tabb, came from southwest Georgia.

Dick was born September 1, 1924, in Erwin. He had two younger brothers, Harry (Wimpy), who is now deceased, and Tommy, who lives in Florida.

The Franklin family lived on New Street when Dick was growing up. He attended Love Street School for seven years and Elm Street School for one year after the family moved to Pine Street. Dick's address when he enlisted was 311 Pine Street. All of his war records were lost when the house burned in the 1950s.

After enlisting, Dick and Bill were sent to Keesler Field (Biloxi), Mississippi for basic training. While at Keesler, Dick had a weekend pass and went to New Orleans. When he got back to Keesler, he found that Bill had been sent to Panama. Bill spent the whole war operating a radio station in Panama's Sandblas Mountains. Dick got to see him one time during the war when he flew into Panama.

On December 7, 1941, Dick was in a movie theater in Biloxi when the screen went blank, the lights came up, and someone came on the stage to announce that all servicemen were ordered to report back to their bases. By the time he got on the street, he heard everyone talking about the attack of Pearl Harbor.

Dick stayed at Keesler as "permanent party" and by early 1942 was a buck sergeant. He saw many men from Erwin as they came through basic training at Keesler, including Lawrence Crain, "Pickle" Ryburn, and T. C. Cornett, as well as Hugh Kyser from Johnson City.

From Keesler Field, a cadre of 100 men was made up to go to Atlantic City, New Jersey, to take over the hotels and turn Atlantic City into a basic training center for the Air Corps. Dick was there from early 1942 until the following fall.

After those months in Atlantic City, Dick was tired of administration work and asked about going to school. His records were checked and school was approved. When asked what school he wanted, he told them "Aerial Gunnery School." The officer said, "You're nuts!" But Dick said that was just what he wanted.

He was sent to Ft. Myers, Florida, where Buckingham Army Air Base Gunnery School had just been built. In those days they had enlisted pilots, bombardiers, and navigators. Staff sergeants and tech sergeants were flying training missions. Dick graduated in the top 20% of his class, so he was eligible for enlisted bombardier training in Carlsbad, New Mexico. He had his bags packed and was ready to go when word was passed that there would be no more enlisted pilots, bombardiers, or navigators. That was a big disappointment.

He remained at Ft. Meyers as aerial gunnery instructor. While there, he saw Cecil Davis, Jr., and Gene Bowman from Erwin. He still wanted to get into the flying part of the Air Corps. When he first enlisted, two years of college were required for pilot training. But that requirement was soon dropped, and anyone who could pass the entrance exam could get into pilot training. Now that Dick was eighteen years old and legally old enough to be in the service, he called his mother to send his birth certificate so he could apply for pilot training. He was sent to Avon Park Air Base, Florida, for the exam for aviation cadet, which he passed.

From Florida he was sent to Sheppard Field, Wichita Falls, Texas. There, aviation students were given basic training. Dick and his group had already been trained and had rank, so they ended up giving basic training to the new recruits.

The next stop was Southwest Missouri State Teachers College in Springfield, Missouri. They attended classes for eight hours a day and received the equivalent of six months of college in four months of accelerated training.

Then it was on to the Classification Center in San Antonio, Texas, then to Primary Flying School in Lafayette, Louisiana. By the time they finished primary, they received word that aviation students were needed for bomber crews in England.

All of Dick's group was sent to 3rd Air Corps Replacement Pool in Tampa, Florida, and assigned to bomber crews. They trained at McDill Field in Tampa. From there, the crews went to Hunter Field in Savannah, Georgia, to wait for new planes. Dick's crew got a new B-17 from Boeing and flew to Valle, Wales, then to England by way of Dow Field, Bangor, Maine, and Gander, Newfoundland. This was in the latter part of May 1944.

After arriving in England, they were assigned to the 510th Bomb Squadron, 351st Bomb Group, and sent to Polebrook Air Base near Oundle which was thirty miles from Peterborough and ninety miles north of

London.

They were assigned a plane which they named *Pappy's Bastard*, in honor of their pilot. The pilot was in his 30s, which was "old" to most of those boys. The majority of the pilots at that time were nineteen or twenty years old.

Dick had only one leave while in England. The whole crew went to London for a weekend during the time when the buzz bombs were the worst. After that weekend, the crew decided it was safer to be flying.

A B-17 crew consisted of ten crew members. At that time in England, there was such a shortage of crew members that if one man was unable to fly, the crew had to "make-do" without him. It was up to the crew to encourage and offer moral support to get the member back in the air. After three missions, the waist gunner, James Dillard of Athens, Georgia, cracked up and was put into the base hospital. Therefore, *Pappy's Bastard* was flying with a crew of nine.

Dick, inside plane wearing flight gear

Dave Strawn and Dick Franklin

Ira Hughes, radio operator

THE CREW OF *PAPPY'S BASTARD*:
    Pilot - Samuel F. Irwin - Mt. Vernon, Illinois - POW
    Co-pilot - Brian F. DeVan - Baltimore, Maryland - POW
    Navigator - Gene Pulliam - Hazard, Kentucky - Killed
    Bombardier - Sam Herman - Chicago, Illinois - Killed
    Radioman - Ira Hughes - Coushatta, Louisiana - POW
    Waist Gunner - Dave Strawn - Illinois - Killed
    Waist Gunner - James Dillard - Athens, Georgia
    Ball Turret Gunner - Charles Miller - Lancaster, Pennsylvania
      - Killed
    Engineer - Zoltan Torok - Steubenville, Ohio - Killed
    Tail Gunner - Dick Franklin - Erwin, Tennessee - POW

The fourteenth mission of *Pappy's Bastard* was a bombing raid over Munich, Germany, on July 12, 1944. The plane was hit by anti-aircraft fire. Five members of the crew were able to bail out. Four went down with the plane.

Those who went down with the plane were Sam Herman, Gene Pulliam, Charles Miller, and Zoltan Torok. Those who bailed out were Samuel F. Irwin, Brian F. DeVan, Ira Hughes, Dave Strawn, and Dick Franklin. Strawn landed in a river and drowned; the other four survived as POWs.

Dick landed in a woods northeast of Munich. When he hit the ground, his legs and back were injured and he could hardly move. But Dick said that is where the training, lectures, and instructions really came back to him. He began to function mechanically. The first instruction on bailing out was to hide the parachute, which he did in a pile of wood.

He was shortly captured by "The Hitler Youth" and "Home Guard."

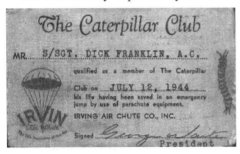

Dick's Caterpillar Club card, awarded by the Irving Air Chute Co. The cards were given to men whose lives were saved in an emergency jump by using parachute equipment.

The first thing they asked for was his pistol, which he had lost on the way down, along with his shoes. Then they asked for his parachute. One of the old "Home Guards" kept hitting Dick on the tail bone with his rifle, causing excruciating pain. After so much of that, Dick tried to find the parachute, but was unable to do so. Also, when he bailed out, he had disconnected his throat mike, but still had the elastic band with two hard rubber discs that fit on each side of his throat. A little pigtail connector still hung down in front, and they wouldn't let him take it off. When he didn't answer to suit them, they kept pulling the pigtail and letting the rubber discs hit him in the throat. It didn't take long for his throat to become blue and swollen.

Brian DeVan, co-pilot, wears a throat mike similar to the one Dick was wearing when captured.

The captors told Dick they were going to hang him. He said they really meant it. He also said he can understand why the civilians were so cruel to the downed Americans. If the Germans had been bombing Erwin, he doubts that there would have been any downed survivors to be prisoners.

Dick was rescued from the civilians by a German pilot who drove up and took him to a radar anti-aircraft gun emplacement battery. (The German pilot happened to be a graduate of Stanford University.) That night, he was taken to Munich and put in jail. After being turned over to the military, he was treated much better.

From Munich he was taken to Dulag Luft in Frankfurt, which was an air interrogation center. He stayed there for twenty-one days in solitary confinement. During this time they took him out of his cell three or four times a day and three or four times a night for questioning. He didn't tell them anything, but he was amazed at what they told him.

His interrogator was a Gestapo major who had been a railroad detective on the Santa Fe Railroad for more than twenty years and had gone back to Germany. He spoke perfect English. Dick said they would sit and talk just like old friends, and it was mind-boggling to hear what the Germans knew about him. One of the first things the major asked Dick was

"How are things on the CC&O back in Erwin?" The major knew the first names of Dick's parents and that his father worked on the railroad.

Dick thinks they must have had some super intelligence system that got information about the boys in service from the hometown papers. Otherwise, how could they have had all that information about him? They knew where he had been in training and all about his base in England.

After the twenty-one days in Frankfurt, Dick was put on a train and sent to Wetzlar, Germany, which he called a transit station where the prisoners were split up and sent to different prison camps.

At Wetzlar, he ran into his radioman, Ira Hughes from Coushatta, Louisiana. After Hughes had bailed out of their plane, he had hidden his parachute and started running for the Swiss border—barefoot. He, too, had lost his boots on the way down. He was captured within sight of the guard towers at the Swiss border. When he was brought into Wetzlar, he and Dick were kept together and sent on to Stalag Luft IV. They arrived there in mid-August 1944.

Dick was the only Erwin man in Lager C, but he was able to yell through the fence to other Erwin men. Hensley, Miller, Norris, and Swingle were in Lager A. Alford and Hatcher were in Lager B, and Edwards and Tinker were in Lager D.

Dick and Ira Hughes were together in Lager C. Ira's close friend was Sid McGhee from Clewiston, Florida. One of Dick's special friends in the compound was Tom Busby from Okolona, Mississippi.

Two weeks before the war was over, Hughes and McGhee decided to escape. Dick and Busby tried to talk them out of it, saying they could easily be killed by the American or British forces who were rapidly closing in. But the boys were determined and actually made it through the lines. Dick still got back to the States two months before Ira Hughes did. Today, Hughes lives in Birmingham, Alabama.

Dick's recollections of the prison camp are much the same as the other men: boredom and hunger. One special occasion that stands out happened at Thanksgiving, 1944. The prisoners had what they called the "Polish Grapevine" or "Polish BBC."

The forced labor workers in the camp were Polish, and they would tell the Americans what was going on. Before Thanksgiving, the "Polish Grapevine" told the Americans that freight cars filled with American Red Cross packages were on a siding near the camp. The prisoners thought for sure they were going to get a special Thanksgiving meal. Instead, the Red Cross packages contained sports equipment and band instruments.

But never underestimate American ingenuity. The men in Dick's lager made the best of what they had. They organized a traditional All-American Thanksgiving Day football game with a band on the field. Many of the prisoners were able to play instruments, so they had a fine band after a bit of practice.

The day arrived and the football game started. They played until half time, then the band came on the field and struck up "The Star-Spangled Banner" loud and clear. All the sports equipment and band instruments were confiscated, never to be seen again.

When the Allied Forces began closing in, the prisoners at Stalag Luft IV were started on the march west to Germany. Some of the men marched from eighty-two to eighty-six days, depending on where they were when liberated. The march covered almost a thousand miles.

Snow was waist deep when they left Stalag Luft IV on February 6, 1945. Dick says they literally walked west into spring. The "Polish Grapevine" continued to keep the prisoners informed as to the progress of the war. The marchers neared Lubeck, Germany, at the mouth of the Elbe River, on May 1, at about ten o'clock in the morning. They were sprawled along the roadside at rest when the German captain in charge of Dick's column went up to a civilian house. He came out putting on a civilian white shirt over his uniform. About an hour later, they heard the British 2nd Armored Division coming down the road. The German captain surrendered to them.

The British informed the prisoners that they were twenty-seven miles behind the lines and that the Allies were trying to cut off any escape by the Germans into Denmark. Therefore, they would not be able to help the men except to feed them at that time.

They were taken to where a field kitchen was set up. Dick said it was so funny, because the men had been used to eating a little bit and saving a little bit. When they saw all that food, they began stuffing their shirts and pockets full. The British colonel told them they didn't have to do that anymore because there would still be plenty in the morning.

The British colonel made arrangements for the prisoners to go on to Lüneburg where they were deloused and could clean up, shave, and get haircuts. They were given new clothes; however English battle dress uniforms were all that was available. They even put the equivalent British rank on the uniforms for each man.

After being well fed and clothed, they were sent to Soltau, a Royal Canadian Air Force Base, where they stayed for three days. The British sent in some Dakotas, aircraft similar to American C-47s, and flew the men to Brussels, Belgium. They arrived in Brussels on VE Day, May 8, 1945.

During this time, the former POWs were under British control. They were turned over to Allied control at Namur, Belgium. From Namur they went to Camp Lucky Strike in France for about two weeks. While at Camp Lucky Strike, Dick ran into George Swingle and Gladys Morgan from Erwin. Gladys was a nurse stationed at the field hospital at Camp Lucky Strike.

From Camp Lucky Strike they went to Le Havre to board ship. Dick returned to the States on the S. S. *John Dickenson*. He said he will never forget the crossing. The voyage was extremely rough, and almost everyone was sick.

They arrived in New York in June 1945 and went to Camp Shanks. From there they took a train to Ft. Oglethorpe, Georgia, where they received leave orders, and Dick went on to Johnson City by train.

After getting off the train in Johnson City, Dick didn't think of taking a bus. Instead he did the usual thing that all the Erwin boys did: He shouldered his bag and headed for the usual corner to hitch a ride to Erwin. Mr. and Mrs. Terry Lundy picked him up and brought him home.

After a ninety-day leave at home, he reported to Miami, Florida. From there he went to San Antonio, Texas, then to Greensboro, North Carolina, for discharge on October 8, 1945. George Swingle, Dick Franklin, and John Salyer (another Erwin POW) were all discharged on the same day.

George and Dick were at the bus station in Greensboro waiting for a bus when A. R. Morgan and Bill Britton drove up. They were driving George's old 1934 Chevrolet turtle-back car. There was room for only two (three in a tight squeeze) in the front seat. Morgan and George rode in the front seat and Dick and Britton arrived in the turtle, which was similar to a car trunk. Dick had really covered a lot of ground from the time he and Britton left Johnson City for Keesler Field, Mississippi, until they arrived back in Erwin, riding in the trunk of a car.

After getting settled into civilian life once more, Dick went to work as a fireman on the Clinchfield Railroad in 1946. He worked until he was "cut-off" in 1948. He then took the GED test and enrolled at East Tennessee State College (now University).

After two years at ETSC, Dick and Elizabeth Charles were married on January 20, 1950. Elizabeth is the daughter of J. O. and Magalee Harr Charles.

Dick finished school at State with a BS degree in business and then

went to the University of Tennessee in Knoxville for a year of graduate work. While still living in Knoxville, he went to work for the William Wrigley Company of Chicago as a PR man.

From Knoxville, Dick and Elizabeth moved to Richmond, Virginia, where he worked for the state of Virginia until 1955. He then went to Fork Union Military Academy to teach school for two years, and from there to Portsmouth, Virginia, to teach at Frederick Junior College for one year.

Elizabeth and Dick Franklin

Dick's father, Harry Franklin, had his first cancer operation in 1959, so Dick, Elizabeth, and the children returned to Erwin to live. Dick was fortunate to get his old job back with Wrigley Company in his old terri-

Rebecca Ann, Dick, and Wade Charles in 1992

— 98 —

tory. He worked for Wrigley until 1965 when Giles Morrill of Morrill Electric hired him as plant manager. He worked for Morrill Electric until 1969 when he took a job with the Federal Housing Authority in Knoxville. He retired from FHA in 1985.

After retirement, Dick and Elizabeth returned to Erwin to live. The Franklin children, Rebecca Ann, born October 12, 1954, and Wade Charles, born December 18, 1956, still live in Knoxville.

Dick and Elizabeth enjoy playing golf and traveling.

Today, Dick looks like a distinguished, bearded college professor—a far cry from the fuzzy-faced seventeen-year-old kid who tossed a coin on the corner of Main and Roan Streets in 1941.

Interview with Dick Franklin taped on November 2, 1991

HOMER STANLEY NORRIS
Service #14037826
POW # Unknown

University of Tennessee football fans have many symbols, logos, and bumper stickers to show their loyalty and pride in the school. One popular bumper sticker is "My Blood Runneth Orange." This is an appropriate motto for the Stan Norris family. Stan, his wife, Edna, and all three of their children are graduates of the University of Tennessee. Edna's father, Thomas Harrison, was a professor at the university for forty-five years. The blood in that family truly "runneth orange."

Let's go back to March 18, 1923, when Homer Stanley Norris was born in Erwin. His parents, Charles and Addie Johnson Norris, were both born and raised in Erwin.

Stan had three brothers and one sister. His sister is Love "Lea" Tinker. His brothers are Ed, Charles (now deceased), and Earl Norris. Charles was in the Seabees in the Pacific during World War II, and Earl served with the 9th Air Corps in England and Germany.

Although Stan was born in Erwin, he grew up in Kentucky and North Carolina. But Erwin was always home, and he kept in touch and made regular visits to his aunts and uncles who lived there.

Stan's family moved to Kentucky when he was two years old. He lived there until he was ten, and he remembers it as a rough and tumble place. This was during the days of "Bloody Harlan" with all the strife connected with the coal industry.

When he was ten, Stan's parents divorced; he and his mother moved to Greensboro, North Carolina. Stan especially remembers visiting the Love family in Erwin who lived in the vicinity of where the State Fish Hatchery is now located. He recalls picking apples from the trees, and the spring that flowed down across the road. A special memory is the springhouse.

In the days before modern refrigeration, the springhouse was the family refrigerator. A building would be built over a flowing spring, and a trough-like structure would be built inside, with the spring water constantly flowing through. Milk, butter, and anything needing to be kept cold could be set into the water, which was always icy cold.

When Stan was in school, the state of North Carolina required only

Stan graduates from recruit training, Hickam Field, June 2, 1941

eleven years to finish high school. Stan graduated from Bessemer High School in 1940. Bessemer was just outside Greensboro, North Carolina, in Guilford County.

After graduating, Stan moved to Kannapolis, North Carolina, and went to work at Cannon Mills. In January of 1941, with war in Europe and what seemed to be the certain involvement of the United States, Stan went to Charlotte to talk to the Army recruiter. He had his mind made up to join the Air Corps and go to Hawaii; he had seen pictures of hula girls and knew what he wanted. Since he was only seventeen years old, he got his mother to sign his papers as being eighteen.

When he went back to the recruiting office in Charlotte several weeks later, the recruiting officer told him that all the openings were filled for Hawaii. The only opening he had was for the Coast Artillery, which would go to the Philippines. Stan says that one of the smartest decisions he ever made was to say no. He told the recruiter that if he couldn't go to Hawaii, he wouldn't enlist. The recruiter told him to wait and that he would go talk to the captain and see what he could do. Five minutes later he came back and told Stan that there was ONE more opening for Hawaii. A few days later Stan was back in Charlotte to be sworn in.

The Coast Artillery that the recruiter wanted Stan to join was in the Philippines during the surrender. Most of those men were killed or made prisoners of the Japanese.

After being sworn in, Stan was sent to Savannah, Georgia, for recruit training for three or four weeks. From Savannah he was sent to New York. He will never forget the trip. The recruits were sent on an old World War I cattle boat that had been converted to a troop transport. The ship's name was the *Chateau-Thierry*. The voyage from Savannah to New York was very rough and almost everyone was sick.

The men had a twenty-four-hour leave in New York, and Stan said he found the big city fascinating. After a few days in New York, the men were put aboard the S. S. *Washington,* which was much better than the *Chateau-Thierry*. It was one of the larger ocean liners that had been converted into a troop transport. The *Washington* went from New York, through the Panama Canal, to San Francisco where the men had another twenty-four-hour leave before heading for Hawaii.

When the ship docked in Hawaii, those who were destined for Hawaiian duty disembarked, but most of the men stayed aboard for the Philippines. A number of them were headed for the Coast Artillery, which Stan had refused to join.

This was in April of 1941. Stan was sent to Hickam Field where he

23rd Material Squadron basketball team, Hickam Field, June/July 1941. Stan Norris is #99 and James Strickland is #66.

had recruit basic training. After the training, he was assigned to the 23rd Material Squadron to which James Strickland, another soldier from Erwin, was also posted.

Stan was assigned to crash boat service. The crash boat dock was located on the narrow neck, or channel, connecting Pearl Harbor to the ocean. The crash boat service that the Air Corps ran was for their own people. They did not depend on the Navy or Coast Guard. The service was mainly for flyers who ended up in the water after combat practice.

In July of 1941, Stan was assigned to the *General Westover*, a seventy-two-foot motor launch. He was the assistant radio operator.

At this time, fighter planes from Wheeler Field were training at a small air base called Haliewa Field at the north end of Oahu. The *Westover* was sent to Haliewa Filed for rescue service. They anchored in Haliewa Bay, and when the training maneuvers were going on, the boat would put out to sea and be on stand-by for any downed flyers.

The *Westover* was still in Haliewa Bay the first part of December of 1941. At this time, the Air Corps was allowing enlisted men to apply for pilot training if they could pass the written test and physical exam. Stan applied for pilot training, and on December 6th went over to Hickam Field for the test.

Stan was still technically assigned to Hickam Field. In fact, he still had a bunk in the barracks of the 23rd Material Squadron. He would have stayed all night at Hickam if it weren't for the fact that the *Westover* was due to go from Haliewa to Pearl Harbor on Sunday morning to refuel. Stan had to be aboard to operate the radio. He caught a ride in an Army truck back to Haliewa Bay on Saturday afternoon.

When the barracks of the 23rd Material Squadron were completely destroyed on December 7, James Strickland became the first man from Erwin to be killed during World War II.

On Sunday morning, the *Westover* was preparing to get underway for Pearl Harbor at about seven o'clock. Stan was on the radio to the tower at Hickam to let them know the location of the *Westover* and where they were headed. The tower told them to stay where they were because they were having problems at Hickam Field. Stan could hear the tower operator talking to someone else. At the time, he didn't know what it was about but later learned that the tower was talking to a group of ten or fifteen B-17s that were coming in from California, destined for Hickam Field.

The *General Westover,* above, was repainted and designated P-11, below, after December 7, 1941.

The *Westover* stayed in Haliewa Bay as instructed. They still didn't know what was going on. The B-17s that were to land at Hickam were diverted to other fields, because they arrived in the middle of the Japanese attack. The crew of the *Westover* was surprised when a B-17 came in low overhead and landed at Haliewa Field, which was a base for fighters. They gave the pilot credit for exceptional flying in being able to land the bomber on a short fighter runway.

Shortly after the B-17 landed, another plane

came in low, right over the *Westover*. It started strafing the B-17 and fighters on the ground at Haliewa. When the *Westover* crew saw the rising sun on the wings of the fighter, they realized what was happening. Spent shells from the Japanese plane fell to the deck of the boat.

The *Westover*, whose designation was changed to P-11, was ordered to stay at Haliewa Bay until further orders. The boat pulled into a river that flowed into the bay. For the next few days, the crew worked to change the bright white boat into a dark camouflaged boat.

After Pearl Harbor, the Japanese in Hawaii were not allowed to go on the water. This posed a big problem, because fish was the main diet of the Japanese. Stan and a Filipino friend, Lantaka, made fish traps and set them out in Haliewa Bay. They went out every day and dove to unload the traps and rebait them. They brought in forty to fifty pounds of fish each day and sold it to the Japanese.

The hotels at Waikiki Beach, as well as many small boats and the yacht basin, were taken over by the services. Stan was assigned to be radio operator on a type of tugboat at the yacht basin, which had been turned into a crash boat area.

This duty consisted mainly of taking PX supplies to the Army and Air Corps personnel stationed on the other islands. They made runs to Hawaii, Maui, and Kauai.

After five or six months of this duty, Stan asked to be transferred to a B-17 squadron that was going to the South Pacific. He joined the squadron as ground crew and was trained to be a photographer.

The B-17 squadron was sent to the Fiji Islands in early 1943 and was there for several months. From the Fijis they went to the New Hebrides Islands along with another squadron. While based there, the two squadrons rotated going to Guadalcanal for a week at a time. There, they made bombing runs over New Georgia and Bougainville Island, which the Japanese still held. While in the New Hebrides, they made daily runs looking for Japanese subs. During this time, the crews were allowed rest and relaxation leave after so many missions. They would fly to Auckland, New Zealand, for a week's leave. Stan was lucky enough to get two leaves in Auckland.

Altogether, Stan flew thirty missions in the South Pacific. One of the most memorable missions was over Rabaul, New Britain Island, off the east coast of New Guinea. The Americans had learned that a large Japanese fleet was anchored at Rabaul. Plans were made to send in as many bombers as possible. Stan's squadron was at Henderson Field on Guadalcanal. By this time, the Marines had secured New Georgia Island and had

Chow line, 31st Bombardment Squadron, 13th Air Corps at Henderson Field, Guadalcanal in 1943

Combat crew quarters, 31st Bombardment Squadron, 13th Air Corps at Henderson Field, Guadalcanal in 1943

facilities for refueling, but no bombs. Stan's squadron flew from Guadalcanal with a full bomb load, landed at New Georgia for refueling, then flew on to Rabaul. Several Japanese ships were in the harbor, including battleships and possibly a carrier. The bombers went in at eight or nine thousand feet for accuracy. Stan says the Japanese were firing everything they had at the bombers, and several did not make it back.

The squadrons stationed at Henderson Field received "harassment raids." The Japanese came in at night and dropped bombs. Apparently the idea was to keep the Americans up all night. In turn, the Americans flew "harassment raids" over the Japanese bases.

Stan told of one memorable harassment: "We took off from Henderson Field about twelve o'clock midnight in a B-17 and flew approximately 300 miles to the island of Bougainville. This island was a Japanese stronghold with an air base named Kahili. Our mission was to fly over the air base and drop one bomb, fly off a few miles, and return and drop another bomb. This went on until all bombs were dropped, then we would return to Henderson Field. The Japanese had searchlights, anti-aircraft artillery batteries, and night fighters to protect their bases.

"On this particular mission, we were over the air base, had dropped a bomb, and were caught in a battery of searchlights. It was so bright inside the plane you could read a newspaper. To escape the lights and accompanying ack-ack fire, the pilot put the plane in a dive. As I was listening in on the intercom, the pilot and co-pilot started yelling and cursing—about what, I didn't know at the time. We recovered from the dive

Stan, kneeling with combat crew in 1943 at Guadalcanal

Stan, second from left, with buddies at
Henderson Field, Guadalcanal, in 1943

Stan in May 1943 at Guadalcanal

Stan visited the Pratt family of Auckland, New Zealand, while on a one-week rest
leave in April 1943. Pictured L-R are Mr. Pratt, Ella, Helen, Mrs. Pratt, and Stan.

at a much lower altitude and headed for Henderson. The pilot then explained that the excitement was caused when the co-pilot inadvertently pulled his parachute rip cord, filling the cockpit with his parachute. The plane had been temporarily out of control while the pilot and co-pilot extricated themselves from the voluminous sheets of nylon.

"We had some good laughs about this later, but it was scary at the time."

Also during this time, Stan changed from a B-17 to a B-24 and was made a tail gunner. The early B-24 tail guns had no turret enclosure, just a seat and two 50-caliber machine guns. The gunner took his place after securing the door to the main part of the plane. He was completely in the open and, luckily, wearing a heated flight suit.

After thirty missions, Stan was sent to Auckland, New Zealand, to await transportation back to the States in mid-1944. After about two weeks in Auckland, he flew to Hawaii on one of the big sea planes, similar to the old "China Clippers." From Hawaii he got an Army transport plane to San Francisco, where he took a train to Erwin. He spent two weeks in Erwin with his Aunt Cordia Smith. His mother had passed away while he was in the Fiji Islands.

After the leave in Erwin, he reported to Miami Beach for about two

Stan on the right enjoys a night club in Miami with Bud Smith, a sailor from Erwin, in the fall of 1943. The waitress and soldier are unidentified.

weeks before being assigned to McDill Air Corps Base in Tampa, Florida.

The time that Stan spent at McDill was not happy. Here was this veteran of thirty missions in the South Pacific, who was now a staff sergeant, having to salute every "Ninety Day Wonder" coming and going. It seemed so petty to him.

After two or three months of this duty, Stan volunteered to go to England as a combat crew member. He was assigned to a crew as waist gunner and assistant radio operator. They went to Savannah, Georgia, to pick up their plane, a new B-17. From Savannah they flew to Gander, Newfoundland, for two or three days until a group was made up. They flew to Ireland for refueling, then on to England.

Several of the planes in the group were lost on the way over because of icing on the wings. This was a big problem when flying the North Atlantic, even though the planes had deicers to take care of the problem.

Stan's crew did not keep the plane that they flew over; they were assigned another B-17. They were sent to a place near Bassingbourne, England, which was a training area. It was here that Stan received his FIRST training as a gunner. They were assigned to the 322nd Bomb Squadron, 91st Bomb Group of the 8th Air Corps.

Stan's brother Earl was already in England with the 9th Army Air Corps. They were able to get in touch and meet for a few hours in Cambridge.

The first mission that Stan's crew went on was one of the thousand-plane raids over Germany. They experienced lots of flack and had one engine shot out but were able to return to the base.

The second mission was in a different plane. Stan doesn't remember if it even had a name. At this time, crews were assigned any available plane.

The crew had been together since leaving the States, but were separated during the different types of training in England. Stan remembers the name of only one of the crew, the radio operator—Harrist from Shreveport, Louisiana. He remembers that the pilot, who survived, was a very young man from New York.

This mission was a raid over Leipzig, Germany, on July 20, 1944. Stan's plane was the last one in the formation, making it an easy target for the German fighters. Later, when Stan ran into the pilot at Camp Lucky Strike, he learned that the reason that they were last in formation was because they were carrying propaganda leaflets to be dropped near the target.

German fighters shot out the engines of the plane, and when the plane began to fill with smoke, orders were given to bail out. Stan could see that the crew seemed to be physically able to jump. When he bailed out, his thoughts were how long to wait before pulling the rip cord. The plane was flying at about 30,000 feet, so the jumper had to disconnect his oxygen mask, jump, and then hope he was low enough to be able to breathe by the time the chute opened. After falling through some clouds, Stan pulled the rip cord and felt the jerk as the chute opened.

As he was drifting toward the ground, a German fighter came toward him. He thought, "This is it," believing he would be strafed. Instead, the German pilot rolled his plane as he got very close, gave Stan a cocky salute, then flew away. Stan thinks he might have taken pictures to verify his kill.

Stan landed in the yard of a house with a picket fence in a small town near Leipzig. Immediately he was surrounded by civilians, most of whom were old. They were armed with sticks, hoes, rakes, etc. Stan was instructed to put his parachute into a wheelbarrow and push it. One old woman kept hitting him in the face and calling him "Luft Gangster from Chicago." They marched down the road about one fourth of a mile and met a German soldier who took over and stopped the beating. They continued a short distance, then stopped and waited until a car arrived with two men who were dressed in civilian clothes with black coats. Stan thinks that they were Gestapo.

He was then taken to what seemed to be the local police station. While there, about fifteen or twenty more Americans who had been shot down were brought in. They were kept overnight, then put on a regular coach-type train and taken to Frankfurt. They changed trains in Frankfurt and were closely guarded by the German soldiers because the civilians were so hostile.

The prisoners saw the depth of the devastation as they passed through Frankfurt. From Frankfurt, they were taken to the Dulag at Wetzlar. Stan was put into a solitary confinement cell for two days, then taken out for questioning. He gave his name, rank, and serial number. His interrogator knew what squadron he was from and much more.

After interrogation, Stan was put into another room with several more prisoners. He recognized one of them as being from his crew, but they acted as if they did not know each other because they had been instructed to do so.

From Wetzlar, the prisoners were jammed into "40×8" boxcars and taken to Stalag Luft IV. The trip lasted for several days. During the trip, they went through Berlin at night when the British were doing some heavy bombing. They also passed through Stettin, Poland, and went to the nearest railroad stop to Stalag Luft IV. It was about two miles on to the camp.

Before the prisoners left Wetzlar, they were each issued a Red Cross suitcase containing a uniform, blanket, toilet articles, and food which included milk, chocolate, and coffee. When they got off the train, they were lined up three abreast. Fifty to one hundred prisoners were in the group. One large, blond, Aryan-type guard seemed to be in charge. Guards and police dogs were at about six-foot intervals beside the three columns of POW marchers.

After the march to the camp began, a signal seemed to be given and all the guards attached bayonets to their rifles. The man in charge at the front of the column began running. The prisoners had to run to keep up. While running, they were being jabbed by the bayonets. The prisoners had to throw aside the Red Cross suitcases in order to keep up; none of the prisoners had the suitcases by the time they got to the camp. Many of the prisoners received a lot of stab wounds, enough to become very bloody, but not fatal. Stan was in the middle of the marchers, so he did not receive any wounds. He says this is the worst treatment he had during all his confinement. He later learned that one of the men counted about forty punctures in his T-shirt and spent many days in the infirmary.

When they arrived at the camp, they were strip searched, and those who had been wounded before and during the march were given medical attention. Stan was put into Lager A. George Swingle, who was also in Lager A, soon got in touch with him.

Stan soon got caught up in the daily routine. First thing in the morning was roll call. Then the prisoners from each building, who were designated for the job, would go to the kitchen to get the buckets of food for their barracks.

Each room in the barracks held twenty to thirty prisoners. There was a small stove in the middle of the room, and the prisoners were issued bricks of charcoal for the stove. During the winter, the fuel did not afford warmth. The men had to rely on their clothing to keep warm.

The prisoners tried to find all sorts of things to keep occupied. They had a variety of musical instruments, including accordions. They organized a band and put on plays and skits. They even had a Christmas program. There was a football team; one of the prisoners had been a quarterback for Ohio State. Another prisoner had taught German at a U.S. university, and he held classes for those prisoners who wanted to learn to speak the language.

The POWs were from many walks of life and were able to share skills and experiences. Of course, there was much reading and card playing. One of Stan's pastimes was playing bridge.

Somehow the prisoners were able to put together makeshift radios, and therefore were able to keep up with the progress of the war. They knew the Germans were losing the war, and so were not surprised when in February 1945, they were ordered to evacuate the camp.

The POWs were put into groups of 500. Apparently they were taken from each compound in alphabetical order. George and Stan, as well as Harrist from Stan's crew, were put into the same marching group. They had known each other and associated with each other in the camp, but on the march they became much closer friends.

The groups were made up and some waited for over a week before leaving, because they couldn't all start out at the same time. The Germans had to make provisions for them to be fed along the way. They were able to spend most of their nights in the big barns on the collective farms in Germany. The barns had hay for them to sleep on, and they were able to find some vegetables—mostly kohlrabi. They ate a lot of kohlrabi. Occasionally a Red Cross food package caught up with them on the march.

When they left on the march, they had only what they could carry, usually a blanket and a heavy GI overcoat. The Red Cross food packages really brightened the days. The prisoners were able to trade the cigarettes and chocolate to the Germans or other airmen for things they wanted. One man, named Duncan, from Arizona or New Mexico, really cleaned up. Before they left camp, he fitted out the lining of his overcoat to hold cigarettes and traded for as many as he could get. He used the cigarettes the same as money along the march.

Stan and George walked together and slept together when they had to sleep on the ground. Two or three men would share blankets and overcoats and sleep close together in order to stay warm. The only problem with getting warm was that the body heat caused the lice to start moving around. The lice had not been a problem at the camp, but once the men were on the march, sanitary conditions were practically nil; therefore, there were lice.

George had been a student at the University of Tennessee in Knoxville, where he was a member of Sigma Chi Fraternity. As George and Stan trudged along on the march, they talked about going to school. George urged Stan to attend UT.

The march did not take a direct route. They kept changing direction according to the movements of the fighting that was still going on. They crossed the Elbe River three times, once going south, then north, then south again.

Stan's group was in a large barn south of the Elbe River. The barn was on a hill above the farmhouse. They had been there for two or three days, instead of the usual one night. Artillery fire could be heard far away but seemed to be coming closer. When they got up on the third or fourth morning, they realized that all the guards were gone. In looking down toward the farmhouse, they saw a jeep pull up and park. Several British soldiers got out and proceeded to make tea. The Americans went down to see what was going on. They were told that they were free and could do as they pleased. The soldiers were from the British 2nd Army.

The British soldiers gave the Americans directions to get to some field kitchens that were down the road. Everyone took off on his own. Stan, George, and two others walked together for one or two miles to a small village where they saw two bicycles leaning against a building. Stan and George took the bicycles and rode on until they came upon another ex-prisoner who was checking out an abandoned jeep. The guy said the jeep had gas, that he could get it running, and that they would just drive it all the way to Amsterdam and sell it. So they abandoned the bicycles and took off in the jeep. They crossed a pontoon bridge on their way to Lüneburg, although they did not know where they were headed.

Along the road they began to see MPs who just waved them on until an MP stopped them and told them that they were on the outskirts of Lüneburg. He directed them to go to the big barracks building that had formerly housed the German Luftwaffe. The compound was now commanded by the Canadians. There the ex-prisoners were organized, deloused, able to shower, and given new Air Corps uniforms. They were told that they would be shipped to Camp Lucky Strike. The planes bringing supplies in would fly the ex-prisoners out.

They were given numbers, and as their numbers came up to go, they were sent to barracks closer to the air field. It was while they were in the air field barracks that they learned the war was over. Probably because of the war's end, the schedule of the planes coming in was disrupted.

After a few days and no plane out, Stan, George, and two others were at the air field and saw a big British Lancaster bomber come in. It was bringing mail to the Canadians. When Stan and the others checked with the crew to see if they would fly them to England, the Britons agreed, so they were off to England! Before landing, the ground control was notified that the plane was bringing in the ex-prisoners.

When they landed, Americans were there to meet them. The former POWs were wined and dined and well treated; they even got more new uniforms. The men spent several days there and were then put on another plane and sent to Camp Lucky Strike.

While at Camp Lucky Strike, Stan and George learned that Gladys Morgan, from Erwin, was there as an Army nurse. They went over to visit with her.

Also, while at Camp Lucky Strike, General Eisenhower came to the camp. He went through the same chow line with Stan and George, although they didn't sit at the same table. After eating, Eisenhower made a speech and told the men that he would get them home as soon as possible. He wanted to know if they were willing to go on anything from landing craft to ocean liners that would be returning to the States. Of course, they agreed to go on anything that would get them home.

About this time, Stan and George were separated, and Stan ended up coming home on a hospital ship. The ship docked in Boston, and the men were sent to Fort Devons, Massachusetts. Then it was on to Miami Beach by train.

Between Fort Devons and Miami Beach, the men were given several weeks of leave called "delay en route." Stan came to Erwin. It was during this time that all nine of the ex-POWs were able to get together to have their picture taken.

From Erwin, Stan went on to Miami Beach. At this time, with the war over and the government trying to discharge the men as quickly as possible, a "point system" was used to qualify who would be discharged first. Points were counted for length of time in combat. Stan thought it would be a snap for him to get out right away because of his time in the South Pacific and England, but his records had been lost. He was sent to Camp Atterbury, Indiana, and finally discharged on September 15, 1945.

Stan and George had agreed that they would meet and enroll at the University of Tennessee as soon as they got home. Stan spent one day in Erwin after leaving Camp Atterbury. Then it was on to Knoxville, because school had already started. He went to the Sigma Chi house and told them who he was and that he was waiting for George Swingle. They gave him a room in the basement. About two weeks later, George showed up. That's how Stan became a pledge to Sigma Chi.

Stan graduated from UT in 1949 with a degree in mechanical engineering. He had met Edna Harrison during his first year at the university. She had been two years ahead of him.

Stan and Edna, left, during a hiking trip to the Smoky Mountains in 1946 while Stan attended UT. George Swingle, right, accompanied them on the hike.

Stan and Edna were married in September 1949. They moved to Chattanooga, where Stan went to work for the Chattanooga Nylon Plant of the DuPont Company.

While at the university, Stan had been a member of the ROTC and had received an Air Force commission. When the Korean War started, he was called back into service. He reported to Montgomery, Alabama, and received uniforms. During this time, DuPont sought a deferment for him, because Stan was working on a project connected with the Savannah River Plant. He finally got the deferment, and the family moved to Dana, Indiana, where they lived from 1949-1951.

In 1951, Stan was transferred to the Savannah River Plant, where he worked for seven and a half years. He was then transferred to Wilmington, Delaware, where he worked in the Plastics Department of DuPont for about two years. He then was transferred to Wichita Falls, Texas, for three years. Then it was to Leominster, Massachusetts, for four years. From Leominster it was Columbia, Tennessee, in 1968. He worked at the DuPont Sponge Plant until 1981 when DuPont sold the plant. He retired from DuPont and went to work for Spontex Company, who took over the plant. After four more years, he retired again in 1985.

Stan and Edna's children are Robert, William, and Jean Ann. Robert is an editor with the *Knoxville News-Sentinel* newspaper. He has two children, a daughter, Kerri, and a son, Michael. William is a medical doc-

The Norris family visited Gulf Shores, Alabama, in June 1992. Pictured L-R: Jean Norris Yeager (holding Barrett Yeager), Martin Yeager, Robert S. Norris, Stan Norris, Edna Norris, Bill Norris, and Jennifer Norris; children standing in front - Harrison Yeager, Michael Norris, Kerri Norris, Thomas Norris, Frank Norris, and John Norris.

tor. He lives in Fairhope, Alabama. He married Jennifer Lawson, and they have three sons, Thomas, Frank, and John. Jean Ann married Martin Yeager. They live in Houston, Texas, and have two sons, Harrison and Barrett.

Retirement years have been busy. For a while, the Norrises took up wine making as a hobby, until it became too much like work. They both enjoy golf, and Edna loves bridge. Retirement has also given them an opportunity for travel. They have been to England, Spain, Hawaii, Canada, and Mexico.

Interview with Stan Norris taped on November 16, 1991

RICHARD GILBERT EDWARDS, JR.
Service #14132520
POW #3361

When Richard Edwards left that big rock house on top of Bogart Hill on March 3, 1943, he had no way of knowing what strange events would unfold in the next two years. Perhaps he paused to look out at the view of the town of Erwin from the top of the hill and think of how many young men from Erwin were already serving in the armed forces.

Richard had enlisted as an Air Corps cadet in September of 1942. Before enlistment, he had worked for twenty months at the Clinchfield Railroad shops as an apprentice machinist.

From the top of the hill he could see his old grade school building, Canah Chapel School, where he had attended before entering Unicoi County High School. He graduated from high school in 1940.

Richard's family consisted of his parents and eleven children, four boys and seven girls. There were many large families in Erwin in the 1930s, and a great number of the breadwinners were employed by the Clinchfield Railroad. Richard's father, Richard Gilbert Edwards, Sr., had been working for the railroad for twenty-one years as a welder. His mother, Lillian, stayed home and "kept house" and cared for the family.

The oldest child was Beatrice, who married Bob Hutchins. Bob died of polio, and Beatrice then married John Price. Richard, who married Charlotte Warrick, came next, and then Kenneth, who drowned in Indian Creek at the age of fifteen. Next came Vivian, who married Blake Brock; Leona, who married T. P. Jackson; Jim, who married Tommye Pugh; Fanny, who married Wayne Garland; Carmel, who married James Freeman; and Wanda, who married Glynn Padgett. Next was Evelyn, who married (1) Harold Luttrell and (2) Bill Bates. Last was Phillip (Buster), who married Alice Vaughn.

Richard had a happy middle-class childhood. One of his special memories concerned a custom at the Unaka Stores. The store extended credit, and practically everyone charged groceries. When the railroad men were paid on the fifth and twentieth of each month, they went in to pay their bill. The store would give the customer a bag of candy for his family. Richard said the Edwards family always received a BIG bag!

When Richard came home for the first time after being a POW, he

Richard Gilbert Edwards, Jr.

brought a box of Hershey bars for his siblings—remembering the old custom. His sister Evelyn just stood and cried and said, "How could I eat this candy, knowing you went without food for so long?"

Richard's ancestry is rooted in the southern mountains. His paternal grandparents, Levi and Beckie Edwards, were born and raised in Mitchell County, North Carolina, just across the state line from Unicoi County. His mother, Lillian Greenlee Edwards, was raised in Carter County, Tennessee, which borders Unicoi County.

Sports played an important role in the lives of most of the young men of Erwin. The saying was that there wasn't much else to do, so the kids played ball. Richard played softball for the Phetteplace Insurance Company in the Erwin Softball League before he entered the service.

Phetteplace softball team in 1942, L-R: standing - Charles Phetteplace, Warren Lambert, Richard Edwards, Junior Miller, Floyd Sparks, Wesley Allen, Frank Stultz, Bus Hughes, and Bill Moore; front row - Oscar Grindstaff, Frank Sams (manager), Bobby Sams (batboy), and Tom Harris.

Richard's first stop after leaving Erwin on March 3, 1943, was a classification center in San Antonio, Texas. From there he went to Ellington Field in Houston, Texas, for pre-flight training, and then to Laredo Air Base in Laredo, Texas, for gunnery school. While in Laredo, he ran into George Swingle. From Laredo he went to Midland Air Base in Midland,

Texas, for bombardier training, but instead was trained as a tail gunner. Richard can't remember how long he was at each of these bases, but each was about three to five months. By January 1944, he was in Denver, Colorado, at Lowry Air Base for armament school.

While in Denver, he visited with Fred and Sue Miller, who were living in Colorado Springs. From Denver, Richard had his first leave to go home for thirty days. He doesn't recall anything special about the leave except that it was good to be home for awhile.

After the leave, he reported to Salt Lake City, Utah, for assignment to an overseas crew. He was in Salt Lake City for about a week, then on to Sioux City, Iowa, for three months of overseas training.

In July 1944, Richard and his crew arrived in England. They were stationed at Thurleigh Air Base, near Bedford, England. He was assigned to the 369th Squadron, 306th Bomb Group. His plane was a B-17.

During the short six weeks that Richard spent in England, he took only one sight-seeing trip—to London for two days and two nights. While in London there were buzz bomb attacks, and he remembers the destruction all over the city.

Richard's crew did not have the same plane all the time. He said they were going in and out so fast that they got whatever plane was available. On September 13, 1944, when the planes were being readied for take off, Richard's plane was rammed by another. The plane was pulled off the runway and the crew was taken by truck back to the starting point, given another plane, and allowed to take off.

THE CREW:

    Pilot - Clayton Nattier - Kansas - POW
    Co-pilot - Johnson - California - Killed
    Navigator - Jerry Weinstein - Pennsylvania - Killed
    Bombardier - Gregory - South Carolina - Killed
    Top Turret Gunner - Gerald Bump - Ohio - POW
    Waist Gunner - Max Kimmel - Indiana - POW
    Ball Turret Gunner - Cecil (Pat) Richardson - Kansas- POW
    Radio Operator/Gunner - Edwin Block - New York - POW
    Tail Gunner - Richard Edwards - Tennessee - POW
    Waist Gunner - Lasseur - New Hampshire

For this flight, Gerald Bump took the place of regular crew member Gene Blaskowski, from Wisconsin, who was in the hospital. Blaskowski had been hit by a truck near the base. Lasseur was also not on board for

The crew, L-R: back row - Blaskowski, Weinstein, Nattier, Johnson, Gregory, and Block; front row - Lasseur, Kimmel, Richardson, and Edwards.

the flight.

The September 13, 1944, flight was the thirteenth mission for the crew. The target for the mission was Meresberg, Germany. The plane was hit by flack over Meresberg, and when it became apparent that the plane couldn't go on, orders were given to bail out.

Richard could not get the tail turret door opened, so he had to make his way back through the plane. He made it to the waist door where Richardson and Kimmel were ready to jump. Richard doesn't remember anything else until he came to on the ground.

Richardson and Kimmel later told him that they were going to let him jump first, but he said, "Hell no, I'm not going." So they jumped. Richard thinks lack of oxygen may have caused him to black out, but somehow he managed to get out and open his chute.

When he came to on the ground, he had been stripped of his outer flight suit and boots. He had landed on the edge of the town near something like a slag pit. An older German man was standing over him with a gun, saying, "Raus," and motioning for him to get up. When he did get to his feet, he realized that his back had been injured. The German kept saying, "Raus," which Richard later learned meant "Move." He was marched into the town, parts of which were burning.

There was much destruction, with rubble and glass all over the streets. He was taken to a brick building and motioned to sit down on a bench. The man left, and someone else stayed as guard. The man came back and punched Richard with the gun and said, "Raus." He motioned for Richard to go outside.

As he started outside, someone hit him over the head with something like a lunch bucket. He started bleeding from the wound. He was taken down the steps, then out into the middle of the street, where a crowd gathered and began beating Richard. They used fists, broken handles, a brick, and what seemed to be a 2×4 board. He passed out from the beating.

When he came to, he was in a big open German car, with a German soldier driving and another German soldier in the back seat with him. Richard feels that he was rescued by the German soldiers, because the civilians would have killed him. He was driven to another brick building, and they motioned for Richard to get out of the car.

As he got out, he was kicked, and this made him fall flat into the gravel and badly skin his hands. They took him behind the building, and he immediately saw Kimmel and Richardson. The two had landed near an anti-aircraft battery and were quickly picked up by the soldiers. They didn't have a mark on them. The guards sat Richard down against a tree.

Richardson and Kimmel did not recognize him because his face was so badly beaten and bloody. When Richardson finally did realize who Richard was, he asked the guard for water. They were allowed to go to a fountain where Richardson washed Richard's face and tried to soothe his wounds.

From this brick building they were marched until about nine o'clock that night to a jail. They were put into single small cells with wooden bunks. The next morning they were taken to another building where there was a large crowd of prisoners. Block, the radio operator and gunner, was in this crowd. They spent the night there, and the next day were put on a train and taken to Frankfurt. When they got on the train, they ran into Nattier, the pilot. He had been badly burned about the face.

They arrived at the Dulag Luft at Wetzlar. It was a sort of distribution point for Allied prisoners. They stayed there for two or three days, and Richard was allowed to see a doctor for the first time, but all the doctor did was clean the wounds with alcohol.

While at the Dulag Luft, they were issued clothing and cigarettes. As

Richard remembers, he received a pair of pants, two shirts, and underwear. From Wetzlar they were loaded into boxcars and remained there for seven days and nights until they got to Stalag Luft IV in the latter part of September.

Stalag Luft IV was located just across the Polish border near Grosstychow. In 1944 and 1945, the camp held between 8,000 and 10,000 prisoners.

Richard's parents first learned of his capture through a ham radio operator. They received two or three cards from different ham radio operators saying that Richard's name was on the list of POWs. It was some time later that they received the official Red Cross notification. They never learned how the ham radio operators picked up the information so fast.

Richard was placed in Lager D with Clyde Tinker. When he first got there, Clyde took him over to the fence and called to Dick Franklin. Dick didn't recognize Richard because his face was still so messed up from the beating. The three were able to talk through the fence during their confinement. Richard did not know that nine men from Erwin were there until after he got home. He knew only of Clyde, Fred, and Dick.

Richard's memories of the prison camp are of hunger and boredom. He worried about what was going on at home. He wondered if all his family were well and safe. He thought of how quickly accidents can happen, because in 1940 he had lost a younger brother, who drowned at the age of fifteen.

During the eight months that Richard was a prisoner, he did not receive any mail whatsoever. Nor did his family receive anything from him. The people at home had to get special letter forms to write to the POWs. Charlotte wrote to Richard several times, but much later the letters were returned to her, cut to pieces by the censors.

The prisoners were kept in a room about 24×16 feet that was intended for sixteen persons. But Richard's room held twenty-four men. The room had built-in bunk beds for sixteen, so the extra eight men had to put their mattresses and what little belongings they had under the bunks during the day.

Most all the POWs were Americans. There were a few Englishmen and Australians, but they had separate quarters. Not only did Richard receive no mail, he received only two Red Cross packages. One was at Christmas 1944, which he shared with another man. The other was before they started on the march to Bitterfeld.

Some of the men in Stalag Luft IV were able to scrounge around and get enough parts to make a short-wave radio. They could listen to the BBC, and so were kept fairly abreast of what was going on. When it seemed that the Russians were about to take over the Stalag Luft IV area, the orders were given to move out.

The prisoners who were in the worst shape were loaded on boxcars, but those who were able had to walk. Richard was one of the walkers. They left Stalag Luft IV on February 5, 1945. They walked for eighty-two days, a distance of about 800 miles, and were fed a bowl of soup once a day. On good days, when they were fortunate enough to have spent the night in a barn, they often were able to find potatoes and cabbage.

During the eighty-two-day march from Stalag Luft IV to Bitterfeld, if any of the prisoners became sick or unable to keep up, they were put into the "sick group." Once when Richard passed Clyde Tinker's sick group resting on the side of the road, Richard said he just waved to Clyde and feared that he might never see him again.

They walked five abreast. Some days they made about twenty miles and some days only three or four. Each man had a blanket and a helmet liner for a hat. They slept in the open with three men sleeping together. They put one blanket on the ground, then covered themselves with the other two blankets. When asked if anyone tried to escape, Richard said he didn't remember any such incidents. By the time they were on the march, the guards' dogs seemed mean and hungry enough to turn on their handlers.

Richard feels that he was able to hold up under the strain of the march because he had been used to walking. When he lived on Bogart Hill, he and his brothers and sisters had to walk to high school and back, more than a two-mile distance.

During the march, he remembered the night he walked to town from Bogart Hill. He was going to meet friends to go to the "show." On his way into town, a skunk crossed his path. He kicked at the skunk and got lightly sprayed. He met the friends and they went to the show and sat in the balcony. Then they noticed that the ushers and Earl Hendren, the theater owner, were scurrying around, looking for a skunk. When they discovered where the odor was coming from, Richard was put out of the theater!

When Richard and his wife, Charlotte, went to the "show" to see *The Memphis Belle* in 1991, they sat in the balcony. After the show was over, they were talking to Earl Hendren's son, Joe, and told him the story of how his father had put Richard out of the theater. Joe Hendren is the owner of the theater today.

On the eighty-first day of the march, as the prisoners marched through small villages, they began to notice white flags flying from the windows and doors. They knew something was up. When they got up on the morning of the eighty-second day, the German guards gathered all their gear together and carried it as they marched into the town of Bitter-feld. There they laid down the gear and their arms in front of the American soldiers. The arrangements had been worked out the day before.

Richard shortly after liberation

Richard said the Americans were the ones who looked like foreigners. They had such fat, round faces and were so neat and clean-shaven.

Prisoners seemed to be coming in from all directions. They were given instructions to follow the four-lane highway about one mile to where a bridge had been blown up and had been replaced by a pontoon bridge. From there they would be picked up in trucks and taken to Halle, Germany. Halle had at one time been headquarters for the German Luftwaffe.

Richard's group was given rooms and fed twice a day in order to get their stomachs slowly in shape to take regular food. From Halle, they were flown to Reims, France. From Reims, they took a train to Le Havre, where they were divided up according to what section of the United States they were from. In Le Havre, Richard ran into Fred, Dick, and George Swingle. Bulletin boards were posted with names and hometowns of released POWs so they could find each other.

While waiting in Le Havre for transportation home, some of the men were able to take leave in Paris. Richard and Miller talked about going to Paris, but Richard was told that he might miss his turn to go home if he weren't right there when his name came up, so he didn't go. Miller took a chance on going to Paris and arrived back in Le Havre just hours before time to board ship for home, whereas Richard had to wait another two weeks before he was able to leave.

When the happy day finally arrived in June 1945, Richard boarded the U.S.S. *Butler*, a troop transport, which took him to Newport News, Virginia.

He then went to Fort Patrick Henry, Virginia, for two days, and then to Fort McPherson, Georgia, for three or four days—just long enough to receive partial pay and be issued some clothing. From Fort McPherson, it was on to Erwin for sixty days.

Sue Miller, Charlotte and Richard Edwards, and Fred Miller pose on Charlotte and Richard's wedding day, July 29, 1945.

Before enlisting, Richard had double dated with Charlotte Warrick several times. They had known each other for years, and Charlotte was a close friend of Richard's sister Vivian. When Richard came home on leave in July, they didn't waste any time. A week after arriving home, he and Charlotte decided to get married. They were married on July 29, 1945.

After the sixty days of leave, the POWs reported to Miami, Florida. The wives were able to go and stay for two weeks, while the men stayed for four weeks. It was a time of rest and relaxation. At one time while there, they were being served a sumptuous meal from a long buffet line. The cooks and workers were German POWs. The Americans were told that they could say anything they wanted to the Germans, but under no circumstances were they to touch them.

From Miami, Richard went to Greenville, South Carolina. The men were sent to the bases closest to their homes. He stayed in Greenville for about two months and was able to hitchhike home about every weekend. From Greenville, Richard went to Goldsboro, North Carolina, for discharge.

Mrs. Mamie Cook was the Red Cross Director for Unicoi County during the war years. The Edwards family was so appreciative of her concern. Each time she had a message for the family, she delivered it personally. The first message was that Richard was missing in action.

When the information was received that he was a prisoner of war, Mrs. Cook immediately went to the Edwardses' home. Several family members were in the garden picking beans. When they heard that Richard was still alive, his sister Fanny said that they all tossed the beans into the air and let them rain down like confetti!

About a month after discharge, Richard went back to work at his job at the Clinchfield Railroad shops, where he worked until his retirement in 1983.

Richard and Charlotte rented an apartment on Catawba Street when they were first married. After Charlotte became pregnant the first time, they bought a house on Opekiska Street that was two doors from her mother.

One good example of the permanence felt in Erwin is that Richard and Charlotte now live in the same house in which Charlotte was born. When Charlotte's mother grew older and needed daily care, Richard and Charlotte moved in to care for her. After Charlotte's mother died, they purchased the other shares of the house from Charlotte's brothers and have continued to live there.

1950s Little League All Star Team, L-R: top row - Coach Sidney Gouge, Wayne Sellers, Jerry Crawford, Lowell White, Harold Richardson, Danny Garber, Karl Lee Justice, K.L. Gouge, Everette Sparks, and Manager Richard Edwards; front row - Wayne Barnett, M.O. Whitson, Tommy Warrick, Randy Campbell, Delbert Barnett, and Billy Joe Blevins.

Richard picked up on his sports activities after returning home. He again played in the Erwin Softball League for Phetteplace Insurance Company and for Tinker's Tavern. Richard was also active with the bowling leagues in Erwin and Johnson City. He was a Little League manager for twelve years, and his teams made it to the state tournament twice.

About 1987 when Morris Epps, from Knoxville, was receiving lung cancer treatment at the VA Hospital in Johnson City, he noticed the picture of "The Erwin Nine" hanging on the wall of his doctor's office. On closer inspection, he recognized Richard Edwards and told the doctor that he and Edwards had been in training together at bases in Texas. One of the nurses put them in touch with each other.

It turned out that Epps lived within one-half mile of the Edwardses' son, Richard M. Edwards, in Knoxville. The next time Richard and Charlotte were in Knoxville to visit their son and family, they called Epps, who was there within ten minutes. When Epps saw the POW license plate on Richard's car, he told Richard he had been a POW in Stalag Luft III.

While at the VA, Epps kept in touch with Richard, and they got together for dinner and on other occasions. It was during this time that it was discovered that Richard also had lung cancer. As Epps recovered, he encouraged Richard by sending him all sorts of cancer treatment information. As Richard recovered, he passed the information on to others.

Charlotte and Richard Edwards

The deep religious faith of the nine young men certainly helped them through their ordeal. Richard and Charlotte are members of the First Baptist Church of Erwin. When he was growing up, Richard's family attended Canah Chapel Free Will Baptist Church. In fact, Richard's father and other church members built the rock church building that stood during the 1930s, '40s, and '50s. The members hauled rock, lifted timbers, drove nails, etc. Richard said his father did the work because he wanted to. Richard

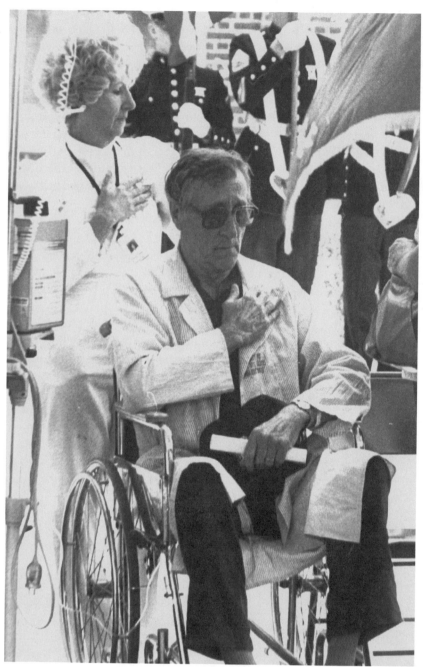

Richard and a nurse at the dedication of the POW memorial at the VA Center, September 21, 1990.

said he did it because his father TOLD him to!

In 1983, Richard retired from the railroad shops after forty-one years of work. He is doing very well after receiving cancer treatment at the VA Center in Johnson City. He and Charlotte are enjoying their retirement years keeping track of their family of two children and three grandchildren.

Above: Cindy, Aaron, and Richard M. Edwards

Right: Robert and Carol Crowder with Eric and Kim

Their daughter, Susan Carol, married Robert Crowder. They live in Kingsport where Robert works for Eastman. Carol and Robert have a daughter, Kim, who graduated from Emory and Henry College and is presently working on her masters degree at East Tennessee State University. The Crowders' son, Eric, is a senior at East Tennessee State University majoring in computer marketing.

Richard and Charlotte's son, Richard M. Edwards, married Cindy Bartlett from Dayton, Tennessee. They have a young son, Richard Aaron. Richard M. Edwards is an ordained Baptist minister and a vice president (Investments) with Dean-Witter-Reynolds, Inc. of Knoxville.

Interview with Richard Edwards taped on August 23, 1991

Richard Edwards died September 12, 1993, at the VA Hospital in Johnson City, Tennessee.

The POW Memorial at the VA Center in Johnson City, Tennessee, dedicated on September 21, 1990, was designed by Jerry Honeycutt of Johnson City. James H. (Jim) Hensley, Jr., was the model for the memorial.

Epilogue

This story is so unusual because none of the men were stationed at the same base, nor were they in the same Bomb Group.

Clyde Tinker was stationed near Norwich, England; Jim Hensley near Molesworth, England; Allen Alford near Tibbingham, England; George Hatcher near Peterborough, England; Fred Miller near Cerignola, Italy; Dick Franklin near Oundel, England; Stan Norris near Bassingbourne, England; and Richard Edwards near Bedford, England. George Swingle was also stationed in England, but it isn't known exactly where.

After returning home and being discharged from the service, the men quickly resumed their civilian lives. Richard, George Hatcher, and Allen went back to work on the Clinchfield Railroad.

Stan and George Swingle attended the University of Tennessee. Stan graduated with a degree in mechanical engineering. George graduated with a degree in geology and went on to obtain a PhD.

Fred went to work for the Consolidated Feldspar Corporation in Erwin and was transferred several times. He retired as a sales representative in Custer, South Dakota.

Dick attended East Tennessee State College and graduated with a degree in business. He then attended the University of Tennessee for graduate study.

Clyde purchased and ran Tinker's Tavern in Erwin.

Jim had his own neon sign business in Johnson City.

Of "The Erwin Nine," two were married at the time they were taken prisoner. The other seven married within a few years of returning home. All nine remained married to the same wife. They all seem to have achieved "The American Dream." They certainly deserve it.

APPENDIX

The following list shows the next of kin and address at time of enlistment for the crew which flew with Fred Miller.

1st Lt. Edward C. Jones - Pilot
Mother - Mrs. Jessie C. Jones
1336 East Moreland, Memphis, Tennessee

2nd Lt. Vittorio O. Russo - Co-pilot
Mother - Mrs. Genoveffa M. Russo
478 South 11th Street, Newark, New Jersey

2nd Lt. Benjamin W. Grant - Navigator
Father - Mr. B. W. Grant, Sr.
75 State Street, Albany, New York

2nd Lt. Joseph R. Woll - Bombardier
Father - Mr. Joseph H. Woll
Summit Station, Pennsylvania

M/Sgt. James I. Sanford - Tail Gunner
Father - Mr. Kent Sanford
East Quorque, New Jersey

Sgt. Walter J. Rogers - Ball Turret Gunner (Belly)
Wife - Mrs. Phyllis G. Rogers
Route 1, Box 896, Bessemer, Alabama

2/Sgt. Ferrell E. Daniel - Top Turret Gunner
Mother - Mrs. Florence Daniel
320 17th Street, Knoxville, Tennessee

S/Sgt. Joseph M. Michaud - Photographer
Wife - Mrs. Leonora V. Michaud
208 Carew Street, Chicopee Falls, Massachusetts

S/Sgt. Jack F. Bonifield - Radioman - Left Waist Gunner
(Replaced Ralph Zetterberg)
Father - Mr. Alfert F. Bonifield
Route 1, Delhi, Oklahoma

2/Sgt. Harold E. Rogers - Nose Gunner
Wife - Mrs. Rosa G. Rogers
4643 3/4 La Marida, Hollywood, California

S/Sgt. J. Fred Miller - Engineer
Wife - Mrs. Sue S. Miller
238 Catawba Street, Erwin, Tennessee

S/Sgt. Ralph Zetterberg - Radioman - Left Waist Gunner
(Not on board for last flight)
Long Island, New York

Stalag Luft IV

This drawing of Stalag Luft IV was originally published in 1950 as the cover for **Barbed Boredom: A Souvenir Book of Stalag Luft IV** by Charles G. Janis. The book was reprinted by Leonard E. Rose, who added the descriptive words.

According to Rose, Lager A was the sick call area, and the Compound Leader was Richard M. Chapman. The other Compound Leaders were: Willard C. Miller for Lager B, Francis Troy for Lager C, and Francis Paules for Lager D.

The barracks in all lagers were built three feet off the ground to prevent tunneling by the prisoners.

Jim Hensley, George Swingle, Fred Miller, and Stan Norris were in Lager A. Allen Alford and George Hatcher were in Lager B. Dick Franklin was in Lager C. And Clyde Tinker and Richard Edwards were in Lager D.